T

& Brian

Thank you so much for
your presence ~ here & everywhere!

Jan

Birds' Eye View

A Travel Guide to the Universe

Donna & Brian,

Thank you so much
for "sheltering" me
with your friendship.
It means * so much *
to me ...

♡ Carole

Also by Ariole K. Alei

AWAKENING INSTINCT
The True Feminine Principle
♥
RUNNING THE GAUNTLET
Navigating Our Way to our Fully Embodied Potential
♥
WINDOWS THROUGH TIME
A 'Possible Evolution' Story
* 'A Trilogy' *

ASCENSION TEACHINGS
The Original Memory
* Audio Cassette Series *

Also by Ariole K. Alei and Colin Hillstrom

HEARTSONG
Conversations About Love, Joy and Sex
Discover the Secret to a Fulfilling Love Relationship

Also by Colin Hillstrom

WHEN A MAN REALLY LOVES A WOMAN
Why We Must Love More
And What To Do About It

YOUR 2ND LIFE
How to Live the Life You Always Wanted
* CD and Manual *

Birds' Eye View

A Travel Guide to the Universe

Ariole K. Alei

♥ HeartSong Solutions™

Vancouver, Canada

Published by HeartSong Solutions™
PO Box 647 - 2768 West Broadway
Vancouver, BC, Canada, V6K 4P4
www.veraxis.net, www.HeartSongSolutions.ca

Cover Design: Jan Rosgen (www.janrosgen.com)
'Energy Drawings': Ariole K. Alei and Jan Rosgen
Editorial: Colin Hillstrom, MaryAnn Hager, Jan Henrikson, Dave Dalmyn,
Donna Chesney, Fran Alexander, Mike Shallcross, Gina Reynolds,
Chrissie Husher, Brad Curtin, Jan Rosgen and other kind souls
Production and Printing: Lulu, Inc.

Library and Archives Canada Cataloguing in Publication

Alei, Ariole K., 1961 -
        Birds' eye view : a travel guide to the universe / Ariole K. Alei.

Includes bibliographical references.

ISBN-13: 978-1-4116-9043-10
ISBN-10: 1-4116-9043-5

        1.   Spiritual life. I. Title.

BL624.A426 2006   204   C2006-903772-8

Distribution: info@veraxis.net
                    www.lulu.com/HeartSong

To all those

who made it possible

for me to write …

Thank You

Contents

Acknowledgments

I wish to thank all those who have played a role and who have supported me to bring this 'book' this far - into your hands.

There are many, and I know that within them - where it counts most - they know who they are.

A special thank you to Colin, who has sheltered me whilst 'i' write.

And to you - for receiving this, for taking it *in*.

Time, Earth, and Other Distinctions

This 'story' spans Time as we know it - and Beyond Time - omni-dimensionally 'prior' and 'post' Time. Within this story there is 'little time' and 'Big Time'. 'Little time' - uncapitalized - represents happenings within 'Big Time'. 'Big Time' - capitalized - is Time as a whole, the container of energy, of 'Creation' - as in 'Space/Time'. It is also the 'turning points' within this container and, specifically, within this 'story'.

Likewise, there is earth, and Earth. Earth - uncapitalized - is ground, soil, surface. Earth - capitalized - is this Planet.

Quotations are used to highlight words in this 'story' which were communicated to or by me. Some of these were 'silent', spoken by guides audible only to my inner ears.

A few names have been changed to respect the privacy of certain individuals. Where these names first appear they are marked with a •.

Foreword

This book you now hold in your hands is the sixth incarnation of this story. It has been written *six times.*

The first Book wrote itself through me in a time I refer to as 'seclusion', when many of the richest experiences described herein took place. The first Book was 'coded' so densely that a rare journeyer, willing to relinquish 'Time' in order to read it, would be able to surrender sufficiently to be led through its pages, cover to cover.

Several years later, I was called to India to 'write it again'. This next manuscript was much more accessible, yet still not stepped down vibrationally enough to be received by most people.

A few years later, in the green of spring, I wrote three screenplays. Boom, boom, boom. One of them was this story. In less than ten days its essence wrote itself through me in a genre I had never written in before that spring.

Last autumn, I received the 'call' to write again. This fourth time the story was again anchored, more simply than the last 'book' version. Yet for a variety of reasons, it still was not 'Time' for it to be released.

This autumn, I was guided to write it as a stage play.

And now, I write it once again.

Each time, I know what my mission is. To write 'the story', as purely as possible, without diluting it. To 'bring it down', into a language which can be received. To tell it, without reducing it.

To successfully bridge the unseen and the seen worlds. To build an energetic bridge, a bridge of words, for readers to cross. To transmigrate, from the shore of slumber, to the shore awake.

In humility, I write again, a simple bridge builder, with energy and words.

Ariole K. Alei
Vancouver, Canada
December 2005

Introduction

Hawks guided me. Eagles led me, to the Birds' Eye View. Consciousnesses outside of form, like pilots, tugs to the great mother ship, led me out. And in. To perceive more clearly the universe as it is.

It is difficult to comprehend – until we are clear and away into our 'no turning back' personal awakening experiences – what this truly is. What it means.

Think of the mind as eyes with cataracts. We perceive with blurred vision. Only when the cataracts begin to heal, to dissolve, do we realize that *what we have been perceiving all along is not true.* We have been believing in a limitation of the world. Our blurred vision has kept our perception small.

Come with me. It is safe. I will teach you – I will remind you – how to discern. This is the only tool – the divine sword – that you need to ensure your safety.

This is your journey, as much as it is mine.

For the awakening of the One is the gradual awakening of the All.

Dissolving inertia. Pulling the mind, the blurred vision ... *inside out. To where it can See ...*[1]

---

[1] In awakening consciousness, one of the first discoveries is that – just as we have five 'outer senses' (sight, smell, taste, hearing, touch), we have five 'inner senses', too. In awakening and utilizing our inner senses again, we begin a journey through a magical vortex. For the 'inner senses' serve as a vehicle to our awakening – our remembering – of all that is beyond the 'physical'. They guide our consciousness into the eternal Knowing of Infinity.

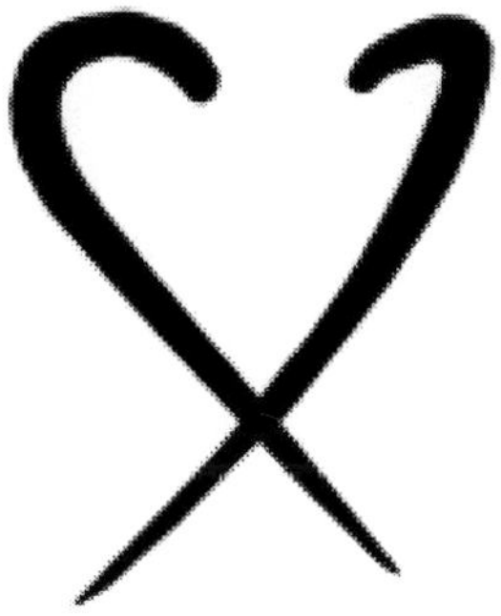

Preparing the Field

I t all began when I was ten.

I may have experienced altered states of consciousness before then, but if so, none that had constellated themselves as clearly as this ...

Eyes closed. Seeing inward.

Me. In a log cabin. Simple, rustic. Red checkered curtains. Then a swift awareness that the *inside* of the cabin wasn't what was important for me to see.

Outside now. Back toward front door of cabin.

Before me, open air. A beautiful, spacious yet intimate, moss covered clearing. Towering, friendly trees, waving their branches in the breeze. Sunlight, glimmering, catching glances through the leaves.

Down, to my left, a gentle creek flowing ... forward, toward the future.

In the centre of the clearing, a table. At which 'I' sat writing. Me, alone, dressed in a flannel shirt. A book. About what, I didn't yet know.

And an awareness, clear, like the thrill of a bird's call held, in crisp air. 'I will live off the land.' Meaning, I will be self contained somehow. And ... 'I will be alone, or with someone who allows me to be alone enough to write' ...

That was the vision.

I never spoke of it to anyone. I was raised in a culture which either didn't experience these things, or didn't speak of them. It wasn't a part of the fabric of our communication. So I didn't tell anyone. Not because I was afraid, or embarrassed, or ... Just because no one spoke of these things.

I forgot about the vision, I suppose, in the busyness of growing up.

Except when it visited me again, of course. Twice. Years apart from each other. Like sprinklings, economical, only frequent enough to be noticed. Like the breadcrumb trail in "Hansel and Gretel". Just enough.

Both times when the vision re-visited me, I was in the company of other people. Once I was at a party, in a circle of people conversing. Suddenly, gently, my awareness was drawn ... away from the conversation, as if it became a silent din. And as they continued their animated discussion, 'I' watched. - The vision unfold again. Precisely as it had done, years before.

Each of these times the vision recurred, I never spoke about it with anyone. It was out of context. There was no constellation of public discourse into which it fit.

So I silently carried it, knowing that there was nothing I needed to 'do' with it. Knowing that, if it was going to come into existence ... it would do so, of its own accord.

Which is precisely what it did, eighteen years after it first visited me.

♥

This is a story of waking up, of remembering, of regaining consciousness.

This is my story, and yet I believe it is yours - everyone's. Use my story as a template. Insert your details - passions, activities, personal events. And it will serve to funnel you open, too.

Know that each degree to which anyone peels open, like a flower blooming, affects us all. We are all intricately woven in this, 'the big ripple'. One system, one energy body. And a beautiful wave of awakening passing through us all.

As you read this story, at times you may be inspired, filled with wonder, in rapture. At times you may disbelieve, doubt its plausibility.

It doesn't matter.

Do your best to keep an open mind. For my mind opening is like a sister lotus to yours. As you keep an open mind to my story, yours will open, too.

If you find yourself at times feeling completely skeptical about what you read, think of it as a fantasy 'story'. Just a story. Like the stories you used to be read as a child. Like the stories that perhaps you yourself read to children, now.

Let yourself be entranced if this arises. Surrender, let go. It's only a story …

♥

It depends how you look at things, what you see. From inside 'me', the vision when I was ten was the first such experience of this lifetime. Yet there had been others which immediately, at the moment of their being an 'event', became relegated to 'forgotten memories'.

One of these surfaced in my consciousness many years later. It was a near-death experience, when I was two.

My breath was being blocked. I was being suffocated. There was something so deep into my throat that it cut off the pathway to my nose, too. I had no other openings through which to breathe.

What I remember is this ... Not panic. Or fear. Rather, the peaceful path of dying.

As the seconds progressed, and my breathing pathways remained blocked, an intelligence within me, beyond my thinking mind, orchestrated the 'folding in'. The closing down.

Moment by moment my body processes were 'sorted' to determine which could piggy back on which. Which were not vitally needed. It was a matter of priority. Similar to the shutting down of the LAM in the movie "Apollo Thirteen". Everything that wasn't needed, one at a time, was shut off.

Processes folded graciously into each other. Thinking folded into feeling. Feeling became minimal. Physiology became its simplest form, like the ameba ancestry from which I came.

Like cards, folding in toward each other, one at a time.

The overall experience was of absolute peace. Simplicity. Increasing stillness. Indescribable quiet.

I was barely a hum.

I felt I was being held ... in an intelligence so benevolent.

Then the breath returned. That which had been obstructing my breath canals had been removed.

And with a 'suck' ... the air flowed in again.

It was, for a brief moment, a shock.

From the quiet again arose busyness, physiological action. And the firing up ... of automatic processes.

Though I accepted Life again ... I had been touched and welcomed by the *peace*.

♥

In my later years I also remembered choosing this birth.

I was energy, spirit, in my 'light body', not currently in physical form.

I was ... in a gathering of peer spirits, like decision makers at a meeting - a circle of wise souls.

There was a hubbub of chatter. I was being ... 'briefed'. Briefed for the lifetime I was about to enter.

Bbbbb ... 'zzzz' ... bbbbb ... 'zzzz'.

"What was that?", I exclaimed. I was being given a list of options, options for the 'shape' of my life path.

Bbbbb, they continued.

"No, what was that?" They paused, a brief moment, as if surprised by my forcefulness. One of these fellow spirits offered an offhanded explanation of 'bbbb'.

"DON'T TELL ME. SHOW ME."

They zoomed into focus swiftly. They knew I meant business.

I was not interested in a description of human suffering. For I was to return as a 'Boddhisatva', one who returns to incarnate existence to assist others to awaken. I knew, for the mission I was accepting - the life path - that intellectual understanding wasn't enough.

For other humans to trust me, they would need to know that I personally understood suffering. I could not come in as an 'expert' - on something I had not experienced, in the flesh, as they had.

My peers in the circle were quiet now. Perhaps they had chosen to take the 'intellectual route' at Times themselves? They were very helpful now, present with my request.

They laid out, in my perception, several 'choices' for my forthcoming human experience - choices of experiencing, first hand, the nature of human pain. Several choices - three, four, five - drifted past my experiential view.

"That one!", I exclaimed. "I'll take that one."

I chose the hardest of them all. To be betrayed, while innocent, by a family member. I would learn human suffering from the deepest breach of trust.

♥

I had another memory ... of the moments just before entering this lifetime.

I was sitting, again as a luminous 'light body', without physical form.

This Time, it was just God and I. The glowing energy field of God was much larger than I. I sat, considerably smaller, next to what would be considered its 'feet', to its right.

It was a very gentle, mutually respectful relationship between us. A very warm, mutual caring. The flow of energy was peaceful, uneventful, until the moment we each knew we must address the 'birth' which was about to come.

God became more serious, like an elder about to initiate a young one into a territory inherent with dangers, grief and loss.

He/She pointed, down, down to Earth, 'over to the right'. This signified where I was about to be born. He/She then traced my awareness, horizontally, forward, through Time.

Within a few moments, a recognition of what God was showing me arose in my mind: I would fall asleep, in order to be born. I would forget God. And the river of life would gradually awaken me, through events and happenings.

Then I saw it, my purpose, my mission in this forthcoming life. I would fall asleep, to awaken. And in awakening, I would affect awakening in those around me, too.

This was it. So simple. I would awaken to awaken others.

There was stillness, and silence, between God and I for a few moments. For we both knew. I was about to forget Him/Her, myself, and all I knew.

It would be some Time before I began to remember … what I forgot …

That was the first time I experienced God's sadness. As I gradually began to awaken, I would under stand more. And with under standing, I would be able to witness God's deeper sadness, and perceive it in the context of *Earth.*

As Barry Long[1] says, Earth is the heavenly created planet. The World is humanity's creation. We can all perceive the schism between the two, a widening gap. Awakening, when lived in action, returns the two into the One, again.

♥

My upbringing was quite normal, as normal goes. I was fortunate to be born into an upper middle class family, with resources and respect for the arts, nature, and personal growth. And yet, as the eighties and nineties began to evidence, 'professional' families had their dysfunctions, too. Just better hidden, behind closed doors.[2]

At a young age I discovered that I could do most anything I set my mind to. I was bright, creative, and physically gifted. I did

[1] A renowned spiritual teacher from Australia, recently 'deceased'. Author of many books and audio-tapes, including Only Fear Dies and Stillness Is The Way.
[2] See Awakening Instinct - the true feminine principle for a succinct exposé of the hidden dynamics of families and societies.

well in school and enjoyed the stimulation of its varied learning. I was curious and enjoyed exploring crafts, sports, and other hobbies. And I was sensitive. The 'voice', without recognizing it yet, was already speaking through me.

I spent a lot of time in nature as a young child. More time 'alone' in nature than with other people, or so it seemed. The truth is that I allowed nature to influence me, and guide me, and show me, and teach me in more profound ways than people did. Paddling, alone with the mist of the dawn, greeting the deer sipping their morning drinks among the reeds. Blue herons, magically balancing on one leg. Eagles soaring, circling, endlessly spiraling. Beavers, sleekly swimming with barely a trace of their body visible in the dark waters of night. And the loons. The loons who haunted me euphorically beyond 'this' world ... as they called across the lakes, across the lands, to each other in the midnight sky. And the moon. Shivering, shimmering silver ... dancing Light on the opal lake. Shooting stars ...

All this I grew up with. It was my cherished 'teacher'. My revered companion.

I was respected for having excellent 'night vision'. I could see - or sense, or both - islands in the black dark of night. I would guide the driver of our boat safely beneath the midnight sky.

I felt very much in my growing years that I have Native blood. I do have a birthmark at the base of my spine which isn't caucasian. There's no definitive genealogical information to prove or disprove this. I simply 'feel' it.

Maybe it was simply living my summers so austerely in the wilderness, at a cottage with no electricity or running water, that gave me this sense. In the summers, the First Nations village swelled to include well-to-do professional families at their cottages. We were among these. I was eternally grateful to my great grandfather for his foresight in 'purchasing' our land. I always felt that we were stewards - not owners - people who agreed to care for this wild and wonderful place.

Sometimes I feel that I'm mourning the past, not so long ago, when Native sacred wisdom prevailed on this continent.

Indigenous people knew how to observe nature - how to recognize the universal principles of 'how things work' - by watching nature. First Nations people knew themselves through the 'totems' of the animals. Their reverence for life in all its forms guided them. Nature showed them its way. It was their 'map'.

East Indian ancients created the healing wisdom of Yoga through observation of nature's creations. The Rabbit. The Eagle. The Tree.

Asian people developed Tai Chi through observing creatures, and the 'patterns' of nature. Parting Horse's Mane. Harmonizing Heaven and Earth.

Eastern Martial Arts evolved through observation and recognition of the principles - the physics - of how energy 'moves'. Flow, force, yielding. All these observed principles were drawn together and taught through Martial Arts.

I remember my introduction to Physics, in grade eleven. I felt like I'd arrived 'home'. Particles ... and waves! Light!! And Sound!! Ripple effects - like dropping a pebble into a lake, and watching its seemingly infinite emanations. Echoes. Surface area. And critical mass. Amplitude. Voltage. Density. Inertia. Velocity. Momentum. The Observer Effect. The microcosm. The macrocosm. Holographs.

And what I realized ... was that physics describes to us, through simple comprehension of the physical realm - *the non-physical realms, too!* The same principles apply to what we can see, hear, taste, touch, and smell with our physical senses - as they do to *energy.* And energy is not bound to the physical. It crosses over, impervious to the 'boundary' of physical or non-physical. Energy is energy. We are energy. Everything is energy. Physics - the observation and study of the laws which govern matter - are a 'bridge'. A gateway for our perception of the *meta physical.*

Altered states of consciousness - subtle and extreme - are simply our passing beyond our physical perception to a perception of the 'unmanifest'.

I had an intuitive realization, at a very young age, that anyone can experience altered states of consciousness without the aid of drugs. I *knew* this.

Interestingly, as I came of legal age for the use of stimulants (and prior to this, 'youth'ful use!), my body gave me poignantly clear, simple signals. It didn't want any. It didn't want alcohol. It didn't want narcotics. It didn't want drugs. Little did I know that I was being 'guided' from within, to awaken as an *energy shaman*. A guide to others along the consciousness path. Energy itself would be my vehicle for this awakening.

And so discovering 'physics' was a sheer delight for me. As if a 'bonus' to this physical existence. It was like a reawakening in me … of 'magic'. It was an inner, largely 'private' experience. Of *wonder*.

I was inspired as a child and as a very young adult. I was inspired by art, and nature, and Life itself.

♥

We are - all of us - in the midst of a metamorphosis. Regardless what theory you espouse to of how humans became the creatures that we are today, you must admit that we've evolved. We've adapted, changed, grown, and in some ways 'matured'. Homo habilis, homo erectus, homo sapiens. Just like the caterpillar which forms a chrysalis to become a butterfly, we too are in the midst of a great 'changing of form'. A meta transformation. Meta means bigger, greater, more complete. Metaphysical: the unseen - the non-physical - is greater, more complete, than the seen.

And so the question is … is ours purely a physical evolution? Or is it essentially an evolution of *consciousness?*

What is consciousness? Unseen intelligence. What is it?

To pass through the gateway of the physical to the unmanifest is like 'listening sideways'. Perceiving past the mental filters. Just as in listening to a new language, direct concentration is sometimes a 'block', an impediment. One must soften one's wanting, one's thinking, in order to perceive.

The unmanifest is real - more real than this physical world. To know it - to 'see it' - is simply a matter of shifting our perception. Of allowing the Birds To Lead Us … Up, To Their View.

Open our minds … to possibilities. Be as the bird. Simply *open our minds.*

Be willing to surrender our attachment to this physical vision. In order to *see.*

♥

When I was a teenager, I experienced words washing through me, as if something was being 'dictated' to me. It came first in an innocuous form - poetry. Prolific poetry. Poetry so rich, and so frequent, that I made a pact with my self - with 'it'. I would always carry pen and paper with me. And no matter what the hour or where I was, when it 'nudged me, from inside', I would write it.

It was more like 'receiving' than writing. It was a process of … 'listening in'. I could feel, I could sense, how it wanted to be written. Like I was its scribe.

"the author thinks i am its feather"

It spilled itself onto the page in a meticulously precise fashion. Which words were to have capitals, and which not. Which were to curve, around the corners of the page, and which straight. Which in pencil, and which in pen. And where, precisely where, they wanted to be placed.

These 'poems' looked like visual art.

Two things struck me about them.

One was that 'I' didn't write them. I didn't think, didn't craft, didn't interfere, didn't censor them as they were being written. And when they were complete - or when I read them again, at future times, it was always the same. I'd wonder … 'Who wrote that?' It didn't sound like my voice. It was as if I had scribed for someone else.

And … I didn't know what they meant.

They were 'coded'. They clearly *did mean* something. I could sense their intelligence. Yet I, at this stage in my life, I couldn't comprehend them yet.

♥

None of this frightened me. Not the vision when I was ten. Or the near death experience. Or the 'dictating poetry, that I couldn't understand'. Each of these was a gentle experience.

In fact, they felt like the most normal thing in the world.

Later, as these experiences paved the way for more 'conscious' witnessing of the unveiling of *Source* - of *true existence,* beneath the Veils of illusory perception - I received this explanation as to how there can be reality - life - beyond the range of our five senses: Dogs hear pitches which humans cannot. Eagles fly directly into a sun that would blind naked human eyes. Elephants sense a storm brewing hours ahead of its arrival in the 'now'.

The 'world' which humans believe in is only a small sliver of what is. If we could expand our hearing to that of a dog, our vision to that of an eagle, and our sensing to that of an elephant, we might begin to wonder at the magnitude of what exists even beyond that.

With the influence of Déscartes and other reductionist scientists, we have accepted 'hook, line and sinker', a very small world view. We have accepted a limiting belief that 'reality' is only that which *humans* can perceive via their five *outer* senses. All else is deemed 'unreal'.

Awakening to metaphysics is simply expanding our perception to more of *what is* - reality beyond the standard receptor range of frequency of the five human outer senses.

The fear of the 'unknown', which currently holds many people trembling in terror of anything which they cannot measurably touch, taste, smell, hear, or see … dissolves … when we realize that *there is nothing unknown.*

Awakening our perception to the larger reality is simply this: waking up from our sleep. We used to perceive All That Is. On the deepest level of our beings, we already know it. Here and Now. It is us who have been 'away from it', frozen, in sleeping Time.

♥

I began dancing when I was seven. I see now how imperative it was to the unraveling of the 'story' that I find such a grounding life passion at such an early age. I needed to be in my body in a very physical, rooted way to neutralize and 'balance' the awakening which was to come.

I believe that this is why - and how - so many people remain their 'shallow selves', cut off from their deeper, sacred wisdom. They are not in their bodies. They live in their *minds*. Yes, they are incarnate, housed in a physical form. And yet they are so separate, cut off, mind from body (and heart), it is as if they are three separate beings. Three beings who rarely communicate. The *mind* is the part of themselves with which they identify, the part of themselves that they believe is 'real'.

Dance was one of many 'hobbies' which my parents offered me. It was like an oasis. Spiritual, emotional, physical, and mental, all in one.

I trained once a week, then twice a week by the time I was eight. By my puberty years I was intensely training in summer schools. By high school I was in professional training. It was an art, a discipline, and perhaps my best friend. What I would later recognize was that it was my shaman, my initiate vehicle, the preparing of the vessel into which *the awakening of consciousness* would come.

The spell, the collective dream, the potion - like a morning mist, lifting.

The Seeds are Sown

I was working full-time as a professional dancer, having toured Europe and much of North America with several dance companies, when the acceleration began.

I knew this sense, this tug, this inner pull. I'd experienced it before. A few years before, when I'd noticed the poster on the ballet school bulletin board, a call for students to Jacob's Pillow Dance Festival. And I knew, without even reading it, that I had to go.

So when this happened again, I recognized it. The inner tug, the inner *knowing.* And I wasn't surprised. It was always *so* gentle, so respectful. Yet inarguably strong.

This Time, it was the Stein Festival. My housemate at the time, Dinah, merely mentioned the words. That's all it took. Stein Festival. Two words, innocently spoken, from her lips.

I had to go. Like Ray Kinsella in "A Field of Dreams", I knew it was a sign. Mine was not to question what, or why. Mine was to follow its directive, and go.

I did.

It was a weekend Festival, raising awareness of the plight of the old growth forest, there in this valley which had been barely touched by human presence in all of Time. It was a weekend of celebration, of education, and of reverence for the First Nations' burial grounds there. And the creatures who innocently dwelled in its streams, and caves, and trees.

We hiked over a crest on a trail leading into the valley - and I was struck to tears by the co-existence of dozens of white teepees and several hundred brightly colored tents speckled among them. Here were sensitive, interested westerners celebrating nature and spirit with First Nations people including elders, children and youth.

I got so chilled that weekend that I hardly drank. I shivered for three days and two nights.

When I returned to Vancouver, something had shifted. A split had successfully taken place, like a surgery. My mind could now perceive two levels of consciousness, at once.

I began to write, a stream of 'insights' into my journals. Realizations - 'Reals' for short.

This was more like an intense flooding than the earlier experience of poetry. It was relentless. Recognitions, awarenesses of how things work, of what is behind the normal human sight. Like a veil was tearing, and I was being shown what was *behind it.*

Just like the poetry, I could not control when, or what, came through. And like the poetry, I was committed to write what came.

It was not convenient. I could not 'shut off the tap' at will. It was changing me, and this was its purpose.[1]

In the mornings, it would flood. As I was doing my daily Yoga practice, Real after Real would enter my awareness. I would lean over, reach for my journal, and write. Sometimes split seconds after returning to my Yoga practice, the next Real would land, like birds in my mind, touching down on water. Real after Real.

Somehow I managed, with agile juggling and deep commitment, to weave my Yoga practice and the writing of the Reals and get out the door on time. The Reals would continue on the bus. And during class, when the company ballet mistress would lead us through our warm ups in preparation for the day's rehearsals. What a challenge then, to hold each new Real in my mind while intricately moving my body with great mental concentration - all at the same time. And as soon as I could steal a moment to journal, the next Real would land, as if a string of jets was hovering in the

---

[1] Its purpose was also to 'anchor energy' - from the unseen realms into the seen. Through my writing of this 'consciousness', even if I didn't fully comprehend it - its source, or its meaning - I was *anchoring its intelligence.* I was being the bridge, the conduit, to anchor its seed, here in the vibratory field of physical form.

invisible skies, waiting for space on the runway of my awareness to 'land'.

This was a fascinating Time, and highly stimulating. I was aware that my mind was being trained to hold perception of the physical and the unmanifest worlds simultaneously. And I felt, for the first time in my life, as if ... 'something was guiding me'. Like an individual, an invisible 'being'. A conscious entity, utterly benevolent, yet not in form.

This 'entity' had perhaps the most witty sense of humor I had ever encountered. Some of the Reals were presented to me in such a nonsensical way that I had to willfully hold myself back from laughing - laughing at a 'joke' which apparently no one else in my proximity could hear.

I was, by miracle of the 'strength' which we all have yet rarely use, able to live in these two worlds simultaneously *and function*. I was being stretched, and thus fortified.

The only 'loss' was that I had no one I could share this marvelous experience with. How could I explain it? How could I describe it?

There was no question as to my sanity. I was actually sharper in my perception, quicker in my body and my mind. It was as if I was suddenly functioning at an even higher level than before.

And so, like a pebble in a pond, its ripples not yet perceptible, a quiet, private experience this would continue to be for some Time longer.

Evidently there was a bridge I had to cross. Or more like - a swamp I had to slog through - in order to 'meet' the bearer of this voice. The bringer ... of the Reals.

♥

I took a wound as a child - a psychic, emotional, spiritual wound, enacted through this physical body - in order to understand human suffering. In order to recognize, from the inside out, the dynamics of human relationships that allow pain to be perpetuated, wounds to be passed on. It was only from the inside that I could understand the puss of the wound. And it was only through experiencing the wound that others would ever trust me to help them transcend their own.

For how can humans trust enough to awaken their consciousness, without healing their wounds? The two are inextricably connected. We come Home through coming home. It is in entering the body - being present with our mind in the Now - that we ultimately transcend it. It is through the body that we awaken.

I had 'forgotten' this wound, relinquished it under layers and layers of denial in order to 'survive', as virtually all of us do with wounds too painful and confusing to address at the time of their occurrence.

The ground was obviously now laid in my life and I was psychologically strong enough for the wound, which I had 'forgotten' in childhood, to be re-opened for healing. Life circumstance tore open the scab. And I could *feel* it.[2]

Life circumstance was as intelligent as it always is. My body acquiesced itself - so that I could awaken and heal a layer of the onion of the wound. On my way to rehearsal one day, the tip of my bicycle handlebar was struck by the opening door of a freshly parked car. I went crashing to the pavement and fractured my knee and hand.

Everyone around me assumed this was a tragedy. Dancer - with broken knee. They assumed that this was 'the end'. In fact, it was the beginning. The beginning of being conscious that I am conscious.

---

[2] There are many, many ways to heal. On some level, consciously or un-consciously, they all require that the wound - which is of its very nature solidified in the past - be re-opened so that it can be released - so that the energy entrapped in it can be neutralized and we, as a result, can be free to exist wholly in the present. In my case, in this instance, the wound was re-opened and I could *feel* it - emotionally, physically, psychically, spiritually.

As my bike and body were in free fall, my 'mind' was suspended in a Timeless bubble - like the text bubble in a cartoon, floating out and away from the 'body'.

These words rang, crystal clear, through my mind. "This is a Blessing. It will show itself, like the spokes of a wheel, throughout Time."

I remarked in that instant that I had never consciously used the word 'blessing' - ever, in my entire life. This was not 'my language'. This was not 'my voice'.

In the months and years ahead I was to come intimately to recognize the *energy* of this message. It was inarguable. It Knew on a level that I could never know. It was my teacher. My invisible, yet highly tangible guide.

My arm was casted, my knee was bandaged, and my face was stitched. With crutches, I would begin to make my way.

Seven days after breaking my knee, I walked again. Nine months later, I danced.

This 'accident' opened a space in my life, a quiet, open-ended Time in which *I could listen in*. My only commitments were several appointments a week with my 'team' of sports medicine physician, physiotherapist, and masseur. Other than this, my healing - and my time - were my own.

I spent hours at home, alone. I listened to my body, to the guidance it gave me as to how to heal it. I practiced my strengthening exercises, and ultimately my Yoga. In the privacy of my bedroom, a beautiful energy of love and peace and faith arose.

Each morning after my exercises, I would sit before my Turkish rug of pinks and moss greens, a tapestry with a peacock turned sideways, displaying one eye. I would chant, focusing through this peacock's eye. Like a funnel, a *'tunnel'*. I just 'knew to do this', innocently.

As I chanted, a miraculous phenomenon began to happen. I was guided, in a similar yet more 'intermediate' way as with the poetry, *how to heal my knee.* It was as if I had been apprenticed - initiated via receiving and writing the poetry and later the Reals - for this. This time, the guidance was a dictation which was tangible and practical to me. I was being given the details of my healing 'map'.

Initially I chanted simply because I felt drawn to. I continued chanting because it *felt so amazing.* The swirling of breath, tingling and spiraling throughout my entire being. I could feel it everywhere. I could feel it - *breath* - flowing even in my toes.

When I chanted and this 'physical', internal, delicious experience opened 'upward', into my awareness of 'dictations', I felt as if an invisible ceiling above me had been lifted. I felt I was innocently tapping into what Carl Jung had discovered - the 'collective unconscious' - a wealth of infinite wisdom, a wisdom 'bank', to which anyone could have access. Like an etheric 'library'.

Free for the asking. Completely benevolent, and with infinite 'vision' - capable of seeing all possibilities.

One morning, I awoke and I 'knew' ... that I would "tour nationally, as a solo performer". I was shown where, and when, and how.

The dances began to be presented to me, like movies on my inner visual screen. I would 'listen in', and I would see the lighting plot. I would see the costumes, too, and be guided where to find the music.

The guidance didn't stop there. It gave me the organizational details, too. It was an experience of being apprenticed, by someone or something which knew everything I needed to know, yet it wasn't a human person, with a voice that I could hear with my physical ears. *Yet it was so practical. And so real.*

If I had used my logic alone, I would likely not have imagined this healing, this creative surge, or this solo performance tour. I would likely have doubted my ability to do all this, even *if* I could have imagined it.

Yet this wasn't imagination. 'I' was not imagining this. I was being 'dictated' this, by an intelligence which was guiding me.

I did tour solo, in the summer of 1989. "there's a camel on my back", a series of five solo dances. Everything was gifted to me, from within. The title, too. I had no idea what it meant, for the longest Time. It was only when I was midway through the tour, and I had experienced the context within which to understand it. 'I have everything I need, within me, to arise to any situation which Life presents.' Just like a camel. I have a 'camel ... on my back'.

♥

Then I met him. The entity who 'guided' me through my healing. And who 'created' the dances, and the lighting and costume designs, and who organized the tour. I 'met him'.

I was sitting in an upstairs room of my aunt's house. It was the morning of my premiere performance as a solo artist. I had done my daily Yoga practice, and my ballet warm-up barre.

I was sitting on the floor, in the corner of the room, about to close my eyes and breathe ... When I became aware ... That 'someone', someone very small, perhaps six inches high, was ... 'sitting' ... just above my left shoulder.

And immediately I knew. I 'recognized' ... That this was the being who had guided me. *This* was the mastermind behind my healing, and my preparing for this solo tour. This was the 'creator'. This was my muse.

I was spellbound. Not just by this experience - of becoming aware and of 'meeting' a guide disincarnate, a pure consciousness, a pure energy. I was awed by its genius. This was the being who had dictated everything through me. I was merely its 'scribe'.

"the author thinks i am its feather"

I had never 'met' a guide before. And I had never consciously explored my 'spirituality' before this. In a very real sense, this experience 'came to me'. I did not intentionally seek it.

So now, here in this moment, we were being introduced.

Within less than one intake and outtake of my breath, this being had 'asked' me. Through energy, as a silent question, posed, inside of me. "Would I ... let go control?" And immediately I was given a physical sense and a mental understanding of what this meant. I saw myself, in the theatre in future time, having 'surrendered, having let go my control'. My feet felt two feet above the floor. Like I was hovering, skimming its surface. My movement was effortless, like a feather being carried in the breeze. And I saw that, because 'I' was 'out of the way' ... a message, an energy ... could be communicated ... from my belly ... to the audience's bellies. I realized that this ... this was where the communication could / would happen. Belly to belly. Energetically. It was something intangible yet powerful, something that could not be conveyed in words. And ... it could not be transmitted ... if I was 'in control'.

I was awed by what I saw and sensed. Yet ... I felt inside me that 'I' had to say 'no'. Not now. Not yet.

And immediately this friendly 'guide', sitting gently and patiently above my left shoulder, gave me a knowing sense that ... 'The question had to be asked. So that, eventually, *I could say yes.'*

I forgot about this experience. I completely forgot it. Until I had overcome the fear of performing solo. Six performances later, and I was in a new city. I had overcome the fear so thoroughly that I was 'bored' amidst the enormity of the challenges I was swimming in. Then I remembered. I remembered what this 'friend' had asked of me. And I felt enormous excitement. Now, immediately, I said 'yes'.

And absolutely true to the energy sense that I had been given - the 'experiential rehearsal' - I danced that evening with a whole body sensation that I was two feet above the ground. I trusted, and I surrendered my body as completely as I was able. I would fall, Timeless ... and a 'hand', a hand so gentle and gracious and huge would ... catch me and ... gracefully ... shift my direction. 'I' did nothing. I surrendered. *This 'hand' ... it knew the choreography even more intimately than I did!*

That evening was an amazing experience. A highlight of my life.

That became the first of many such amazing experiences. Phenomenal, one-of-a-kind experiences whose purpose was to wake me up *to energy. To the brilliance of disincarnate intelligence.* One at a time, these intelligences and these guided experiences would lead me out on a limb. A limb of letting go my attachment to the 'seen', to the felt, to the heard physical world. And in letting this go, I would begin to perceive again, in all its radiant glory, the reality of *'what is beyond ... this'.*

♥

My inner guidance had told me very clearly 'not to tell anyone'. That I would heal my knee. That I would tour solo.

It explained to me, very patiently, that ... people would doubt me. They would perceive it as my wishful thinking talking. They would think that I was deluding myself. That my career was over, and that I was hallucinating, dreaming of a miracle in order to avoid my professional 'death'.

I understood how they could believe this.

Yet *I* knew that what I was experiencing was true. The guidance leading me from within - the visions, the voices - they were completely benevolent. I *knew* that they were leading me 'to'. To my deeper truth. I trusted them more than, perhaps, I had trusted any body in the flesh. Because they had no ulterior motive. Other than to awaken me, as I had agreed to, prior to my birth. And in so doing, to 'use' me, to awaken others, too.

And so my inner guidance had gently suggested to me ... that I tell no one of the extent of my premonition of my healing or of my return to the stage - until I had done it. They explained to me that ... I was an 'experiment'.

As they said this, I could sense the fragility of my recovery, and of my faith in it. I could sense the tender fragility of this 'operation' - their communicating with me, my accurately receiving their guidance, and my trusting it and them more than the 'seen' world. More than human doubt.

This 'experiment' ... was guidance itself.

When I completed my first solo tour - when I had successfully performed five consecutive solo dances in eighteen performances in three cities - with a 'broken knee'. And having never been officially 'apprenticed' in any or all of these new roles[3] that I, with immediate success, played. (At least, not by a human!!) When I accomplished this 'miracle', many people were eager to know ... How? How had I done it? This miracle?

It was safe then. The experiment was complete. It was successful. Now I could tell them. Now I could answer to their curiosity.

I told them that I had been guided. I told them of the visions, and the voices. Of 'seeing' the solo dances, in my inner mind. They

---

[3] Performing solo, choreographing, artistic directing, tour managing, lighting designing, costume and props designing ...

couldn't deny me then. I had done it. I had created a 'miracle', and this intrigued them …

I revisited my delightful sports medicine specialist. I asked him, "So, Doctor Doug. What was my prognosis?" And he said to me, with an incredulous grin, "You weren't to walk again, without a limp."

We laughed together. He had wisely known to not tell me the limited prognosis that his medical science had predicted. Because he knew … that the make-or-break ingredient in mine and anyone's healing … was the *power of my will.*

In my case, aligning with my true will was like dialing direct to divine guidance.

… Or did it dial me?!?

♥

Once my inaugural solo tour was complete - with full houses, hot audience 'must see' buzzes, and great reviews - everyone around me assumed that this was the 'beginning'. The beginning of my making it big as a solo dancer.

Inside of me though, I felt that to continue in this direction was to push in vain against a concrete wall. 'Spirit' was getting simpler, more direct (or I was perceiving it much more easily) in the ways in which it spoke to me. I was beginning to 'feel energy'. And

I was recognizing that this energy, itself, was a message to me. With this recognition, I was able to go into stillness, and *understand its - energy's - meaning.*

My guidance spoke to me through energy itself. The movement of it. The void of it. The stillness of it. This was its 'language'. This is how it spoke, and how I learned to hear it.

So experiencing my body like a limp pool on the studio floor, and perceiving forward motion to be towards an immovable concrete wall - I knew. I knew to ask the question. 'What did this mean? What was guidance communicating to me?'

The answer came, as it always does, simply and sublimely. *"Let go dance."*

Everyone thought I was crazy. At the height of my career. With so much there, on the horizon. Yet this message, so plain and so clear, brought me so much relief. I was tired, emotionally tired. I had danced since I was seven. I had 'perceived the world, through the filter of dance'. I felt so refreshed at the possibility of exploring the world in other ways. 'How did other people think?', I wondered. 'How did other people perceive the world?'

With the 'let go dance' message there was more guidance. Crystal clear. "You will dance again, stronger than ever before. You will know when, and where, and why."

So this was to be a 'temporary retirement'. This made it so easy to let go.

And ... something else ... about ... 'spirituality'. That I needed to become stronger ... spiritually. That ... the world, and I, were not ready, yet. For the potency of energy, which was beginning to flow through me, through the dances.

For half a day, I felt lost. Who was I? What would I do? By afternoon, the energy within me was flowing. The river within me was speaking to me, guiding me anew.

In these fledgling days of newness I wondered, in my still naiveté ... What could possibly follow this? What could possibly be more challenging, or more inspiring and exciting, than what I had just done? In the months immediately following my inaugural solo tour I described it as "The most challenging - and rewarding - experience of my entire life."

And so I assumed that this had been my gem. That this had been it, the one. I had been given this amazing opportunity. Surely the remainder of my life would be therefore 'normal', somewhat bland. I couldn't imagine anything more miraculous than this. And ... even if there existed some other marvel ... surely I had had my share.

Within a few months I was to realize: that this, my inaugural solo tour, and the healing which preceded it - it was merely a 'rehearsal'. It was an apprenticeship, a practice, a training. For trusting in spirit - invisible guidance. And being *led*.

Sprouting Seeds

I thought I was going to become a physiotherapist. Something 'normal'. A profession which spoke the language of the world. A popular profession. I thought I was going to become 'like the world'.

I received a $17,000 grant, which I sent back. I sent it back - just like I returned my university texts - because my 'guidance' led me to.

It had been barely nine months since my last performances and the crystal clear voice entreating me to 'Let go dance'. I had worked in a café, a 'delightful new experience of the world'. I had enjoyed it, and been praised by the owners as an 'ideal person to work with them', until … Until the experience began to shift, from inspiring to deflating. Until the negativity and gossip and moroseness of some of the long-time staff began to wear me down. Until I was about to be pulled into the downward spiral of resentment and hurt - the world of so many workers of the world.

The day that I realized I was on this threshold, I left. I left in order to maintain my positivity.

I worked in that environment so that I could see the downward spiral, to realize that it is us - it is up to us - to make decisions which keep us spiraling up.[1]

So summer was done and autumn was near. I was due to pay the final installment of my tuition for physiotherapy at university.

I was on my bicycle, doing a series of errands downtown. One of them was to pay my tuition at the bank. Any bank would do. I had plotted my path, envisaging which bank I would stop at.

That's funny, I thought to myself. I normally have an excellent memory and yet … I just cycled right past the bank I was intending to stop at! Bemused, I envisaged the next bank along my route. I would stop there.

Again, I somehow cycled right past it. And again, I envisaged where the next bank was. I forgot three times!! I 'forgot' … ?

I began to sense that something uncanny was taking place. That 'I' was … being assisted to forget! I accepted what was - that there were no more banks along the way, and I cycled home. Once inside the tranquility of my home, I lay down, and I *asked in.*

---

[1] See www.veraxis.net for 'Life Spiral Solutions', a personal Coaching practice which elucidates this.

I had learned, through the process of healing my knee and preparing for the solo tour, to *lie down*. I had learned that - at least for me - lying on my back on the floor was the most restful position for my body. And that, when my body was ultimately relaxed, my mind could be still. This stillness was vital for the 'quietness'. In this quietness, I could ask questions inward. And I could hear, or feel, a clear response. This was how I learned to work *with* my guidance. To make myself available for it to speak to me.

So there I was, lying on my bedroom floor, yet again. This time, asking inwardly, 'What is going on here?!??' As if praying inwardly, asking an intelligence which I knew could and would communicate to me, from inside the stillness of my self. 'Why was I stopped - from paying my full tuition?'

A wave of sensation immediately washed over and through my body. And with it I 'knew'. I wouldn't be going to university. Yes, I had perceived accurately, I would be 'learning'. Yet not at a 'physical institution'. Not at a '3D' learning place. I would be studying. Just not at a traditional school.

I sat up, and leaned against my bed. If I wasn't going to school next Monday morning ... what would I be doing? What would be my life 'map'? And an energetic voice rang through me. I will get up. And I will know what is the first thing I am to do. And in doing it, I will know the next. And through it, the next. *I will be led.*

This was a whole new development - an extension of trusting the healing of my knee, and the solo tour which opened out from it. For this next phase of 'Time', I would have no familiar construct. No familiar container.

This day was the beginning of my trust. My real trust. I let go the reins. I let go the ideas of who I was and what I was here to do. I allowed the 'description of me' - my cultural identity - to no longer be all important, clearly defined. Little did I know, I was being led just like an initiate of an ancient culture. Led into the sacred teachings. Led as a young shaman would be led. And yet, with no recognition of this way of teaching in the white western world, I was entering 'no man's land'. I was leaving the world of convenient definitions. Identifiable roles. Ego markers.

I had no fear. I followed the thread, the golden light inside of me. I let the 'invisible intelligence' … lead me.

♥

The next few months were accelerated Time. I had no schedule, no commitment to others, to the constructed world. So I was entirely free to flow with the 'schedule' which my guidance created for me, day to day, moment to moment.

I was free to meet, to encounter, to wonder and to wander, to receive transmissions, to be quantumly lifted into realms of awareness which were still mild and simple, yet already well beyond the contemplation of the normal western world. It was as if I was gaining altitude, learning to fly with the birds.

I began to realize that none of these experiences were repeated. No two were the same. This 'training' was sleek, no energy or Time wasted. As the purpose of the training was to fortify my trust, no experience was ever duplicated to 'validate it'. One was all I got. One was apparently enough.

There were dozens of them, within a two month period. Often three experiences of 'teaching', of altered states of awareness, in one day.

I had one friend during this acceleration. Sue. We recognized that being together grounded us and thus allowed for a quantum acceleration. Our presence and proximity to each other catalyzed each of us in a remarkable way, as if we were 'amping each other up'.

The experiences which we each 'individually' beheld took place so fast that we couldn't possibly share and discuss them all. Yet ... being together allowed an anchoring, a grounding which enabled us both to awaken so quickly, and in such a short phase of Time.

To describe all of these experiences would be like writing a mini encyclopedia. I'll share a few of them here.

I encountered a young man who was a Tarot reader. He sensed he was on the threshold of a new gift – a gift of leading others into memories of their past lives. He was seeking the first people whom he would explore this with.

We sensed a synergy between us. I hadn't consciously wondered about my past lives before, and yet it seemed that we were being brought together for a reason. So we set a time, and I met him at his house. We settled in his living room, I seated on the sofa, he in an armchair. And we began.

I must admit that in the first few moments I felt a fear - an unfamiliar fear - of being impotent! What if ... nothing happened? What if ... I didn't remember anything? Then suddenly, as if a warm golden lava stream flowing from an unquestionable source, I began to remember ... Three past lives, as if triplets, birthed one after the next. They arrived into my awareness that afternoon.

First I saw a luminous white sea, vast and infinite. Then a small rowboat, riding the waves toward a shore. This was me. I was watching me. I was a young maiden, in a white dress, with long golden locks. I was the daughter of a captain of a ship, further out to sea.

As my rowboat alighted on the sandy shore, I was greeted by barely clad men, women and children - people of a warm climate culture. In my innocence I had no fear. I allowed myself to be greeted and welcomed by them as if I knew who they were.

They led me away from the shore, and gestured to me their desire that I lie down with my back on the red earth. I did.

They lined themselves on either side of me, kneeling. Beyond those flanking me, others stood. I was completely surrounded. Those standing masked the light of the sun, and I was cast in shadow.

They began scooping into me, carving out my flesh and organs, eating me alive.

Suddenly my inner vision shifted. I was no longer watching the live sacrifice of 'me'. It was as if the movie rewound itself, and I was arriving at the shore again. This time, after I was asked to lie down on the bare earth and they surrounded me, I sat up. I began to communicate with them, in grunts and sounds from deep in my belly. They responded. They began to smile, one and swiftly all of them. Our communication became festive, animated. This time no one ate me. It wasn't even a concept in their minds.

It was time for me to leave. With this recognition, a wave of unspoken sadness swept over us all. It was a sweet sadness, a sadness of accepting our imminent parting. We had become friends.

They walked with me - the adults with the children playing all around us - to where the ocean meets the sand. There awaited my rowboat. Our parting was sweet and warm. We had discovered each other.

I climbed into my rowboat and began rowing into the waves until they carried me out to sea.

I had met these strangers, and we had become friends.

♥

There was barely a pause, when the next memory began to flow into my awareness. It seemed symbolic, more than literal. Somewhat like the young maiden in the rowboat memory. Like the *metaphor* at the heart of it was the most important aspect of what I was being shown.

I was standing on a precipice of rock, a 'V' protruding from the height of a cliff. It extended out, like a 'lip' overlooking a deep valley. Gazing out, this valley extended long ahead of me, its green walls rising high and wide on either side for a seemingly infinite distance. Like a rich green echo ...

Once I recognized my surroundings, I became aware of the presence of a man beside me, to my left. I recognized his essence - not his name, or his face - for these details, I knew, would be different the next Time I met him. I recognized that the purpose of this vision, this memory, was to remember his *essence*. This was a signpost, something which I was to imprint, *so that I would recognize it*. So that I would recognize him, when he appeared again.

I felt such complete trust in him. Like I could trust anything and everything in him, because he was this trustworthy. I realized in this moment that I hadn't met anyone yet, in this lifetime, whom I could trust so deeply as him.

I recognized him as being an archangel Gabriel essence, though I didn't know the word 'Gabriel', yet. Just its essence. It was 'dark hair'. It was a particular kind of *energy*. To trust it, for me, was rare.[2] This man. I would meet again *this man*.

Several years later, I did. It was Pedro •. It was Pedro I had seen in this 'vision'. He was being 'bookmarked' in my awareness. Signposted. I was being prepared. To recognize him when I 'met' him. I was being prepared … to meet Pedro, again.

♥

The third vision followed swiftly on the second. I first became aware of an enormous, blinding white light. Like a floodlight in a football stadium.

As soon as I registered this - as soon as I acknowledged internally that I could see it - it shifted. Like a zoom lens, it drew inward. Now, it was the bright light of an operating table. And it

---

[2] I am a Michael essence. Michaels and Uriels are typically at ease with each other in the depth of their beings - like soul mates, 'cut of the same cloth', split from the same diamond *Source*. Likewise, Gabriel and Mother - 'Raphael' - energies are most akin.

was over me! Again, as soon as I registered this awareness, it shifted.

I was seeing a square now, in the centre of an ancient town. I sensed 200, 300 years ago. The ground was a dusty, red clay. The 'lens' kept narrowing in, focusing in, with each stage of my recognition of what I was seeing.

'Pow, pow'. It was as if ... I could *feel* something now. The sound, this strange sound, drew my attention to its sensation. 'Pow, pow'. My skin, the surface of my body, like the blubber of a whale. 'Pow, pow'. They were stones! And my awareness of their full impact was being shielded by this sensation of my skin being like blubber. 'Pow, pow'. I was being stoned!

Then I noticed them. The people. Hundreds of them. Milling aggressively around me. Some onlookers, some throwers.

And at that very moment, as if I had noticed enough ... *my consciousness began to lift up.* My awareness began to rise ... up ... and out ... of the crown of my head, ascending above my body. As it floated upward, beyond 'them', well above the buildings, and the trees ... I could look down ... from up. I had turned 180° in my view.

A great sigh washed through me now. 'Down there' ... 'they' ... were 'stoning me'. 'They' thought ... that they could kill 'me'. Yet from this vantage, this height from which I now viewed the stoning, I knew. That they could destroy my body. Yet they could never, ever kill 'me'. They couldn't even scratch my soul.

And the *wave of compassion* which washed through me. I, Ariole, had never experienced anything like this emotion before. Nothing in this lifetime came near it. Not love. Nor forgiveness as I had known these emotions in this lifetime could compare. A wave of such empathy and forgiveness washed down from me to where the throngs of people were stoning my body. I forgave them. Fully and completely, as if the waters of a great birth were washing out from me.

For, from where I witnessed this, I remembered. I knew. I was a 'white witch'.[3] And they were stoning me because they were afraid. They didn't understand what I meant by what I said, by how I lived, by what I taught. They didn't understand ... and so they were afraid.

I under stood this, and them. And I forgave. Tapped into an infinite Source of Divine Compassion[4], I completely forgave them.

My soul left my body. 'I' was whole, and safe.

---

[3] The term 'witchcraft' is usually equated with malevolent practices intended to harm. 'White witches' were / are individuals who work with the power of Light - of consciousness - to effect healing and awakening for themselves, others, and ultimately All That Is.

[4] Divine Compassion is an attribute of the greatest possible consciousness. It Knows everything - pain, truth, joy, slumber - and it Loves and Forgives from this limitless state of awareness.

Just before I 'awoke' from the past life regressions, a crystal clear voice spoke. "This Time the ending's different. This Time, the ending's different."

It didn't need to explain. I immediately knew what this meant. This time, I won't be killed for who I am.

I felt relief - and an awakening of dormant fear. On the one hand, this crystal clear message was the ultimate assurance. I won't be killed this time.

At the same time, it was awakening me, stirring me from my innocence, to the gauntlet I was about to walk. Not a gauntlet that was 'real'. (Or so the 'voice' so valiantly promised me.) A gauntlet that I would imagine. - How could I discern? Would the gauntlet merely be my own fear?

I would have to trust this voice - trust that *it knew* the Truth - the ultimate discernment of my safety. I would, as my awakening would lead me, walk into the path of former fear. Territory in which I had been persecuted before. I would test the message of this crystal clear voice, with my life.

♥

I experienced - in this body, this lifetime's body, here, now - a wave of Love so profound. Similar in its purity and amplitude to the Forgiveness which 'she' emanated, the me in the stoning lifetime.

It opened up, blossoming like a bud, unfolding, and lasted several days.

It emanated from my chest and arms. It washed through me, and out from me, as if I was a conduit for a divine Mother energy. She was Love.

Numerous people received this Love, as I was drawn to hug them. They swam in its wash, like babies in The Mother's arms.

One of these encounters opened my eyes to Love here on Earth. And humans' misperception of it.

I had recently encountered Tomas - one of the myriad new connections which were being made in this 'acceleration' phase - as if a relay, and we were passing transmissions to each other. We would meet, exchange some wisdom, and be gone. So quickly sometimes it seemed like a dream.

Tomas had asked me to meet him for tea. He had sensed something about me, and he wanted to ask me some questions. I agreed. We met at the Naam café.

We chatted for some time, me responding to his questions from a wisdom which was part mine and part channeled. It effortlessly flowed.

When it was time to leave we stood, and I offered to hug him. He wouldn't let go. It was as if he had plugged into a source so strong that he refused to release it, for fear that he wouldn't find it again. Gradually and discreetly I released myself from his grip, and drew away.

I bid him farewell, as gently as I could, knowing that I was being shown something important for me to under stand.

When I was alone again, I listened in. It was this. Humans' experience of love is so diluted from the Love which is available to them. Being cut off from their perception of the invisible realms, they are hence cut off from this Love - or so it seems. To reach this Love, they must surrender their minds - their attachment to the limitations of the physical world. This Love is numinous. It is other worldly.

I realized that Tomas had mistaken this Love for sexual love. As I listened in, I realized that the most fulfilling, enriching love which most humans knew and were familiar with *was* sexual love. And so they assumed that sexual love was the ultimate Love.

It is difficult to describe this - the plummeting feeling in my heart, when I realized the sadness of this situation. It is as if humans are longing to drink from the vine, yet they mistake a dried up, shriveled root as the Source.[5] They seek what they cannot find.

♥

---

[5] Pure sexuality is a powerful Love and can be a direct link in awakening to the Divine. And yet the 'sexuality' which is sold and bought daily in our worldly perceptions is, for many / most people, a far cry from Divine Love.

I was sitting in the living room. I had already prepared my pack, with tent and food and hiking boots. Sue - the one friend with whom I could speak freely about my experiences during this accelerating time - was out doing a last errand. When she returned, we would drive to the foot of the trail for a hike to Garibaldi Lake.

As I waited for Sue, sitting in stillness and silence ... I began to see a vision. I followed it, as it led me in my inner mind.

It was up, at the top of the trail (a place I had never been to before). The land was delicate - gnarly trees barely taller than myself. Tiny plants, moss and lichen at my feet.

The delicate, narrow trail wended its way to the first clear view of the lake. When the trail arrived at the beginning of the wilderness campground, it veered along the lakeshore to the right. My *vision* led me left.

It showed me a private campsite, set away from the rest. It stood alone, solitary. It was down, toward the left, sequestered from the others, at the very rim of the lake.

I sat there, on the sofa, in the silence, wondering what this vision meant. I knew it was a 'test'.

Sue entered, buoyant and jovial as always. She was ready. We loaded our gear into her car, and left.

Several hours up the trail, carrying full backpacks, we came to a fork in the trail bearing a sign. It said 'Garibaldi campsite full. Take Taylor Meadows site'. We were stunned. We both had had a strong sense - a pull - to hike to Garibaldi Lake. The sun was beginning to set. If we continued to our planned destination, at the pace at which we could ascend with our full packs, we'd arrive at dark. There wouldn't be enough dusk light to retrace our steps to this junction to take the Taylor Meadows path.

Logic would have had us follow the instructions of the sign. Yet ... the 'test'. The vision had come to me, so clearly ... as a 'test'. Sue agreed. We must follow the vision. We would proceed ahead, to Garibaldi Lake.

We arrived at the foot of the campground, just like in my vision. There was barely a glimmer of light left in the sky. Dusk was quickly slipping into dark. In that instant a Warden came toward us on the trail. "Campsite's full, ladies", he sang in his elated voice. Who wouldn't be joyous, I thought, working and living in this pristine place all summer?

We each felt a pang of fear cut through our chests. Then, without missing a beat, he said, "But you're in luck. There's one overflow site left". And he pointed, down toward the left, to exactly the site I had been shown in my vision.

Exactly the site.

We never did tell him the magnitude of our situation. That a vision had led us here, to this very site. It wouldn't have meant much to him, perhaps. But to us, it was another step in the strengthening of our trust.

♥

It was during that weekend at Garibaldi Lake that I became aware of two things: how few people there were with whom I could speak about my profound experiences - how 'small' my social world seemed to become, with each new psychic phenomenon. And ... how bright a light I was beginning to emanate.

Sue could see it. Sue could see a lot of 'invisible' things.

I began to wonder if others could, too.

♥

I had a vision of myself walking, along the streets and sidewalks of New York City, towering skyscrapers like enormous vertical banks beside me.

I was dressed in a designer, asymmetric outfit. It was a very, very precise shade of blue. The design wasn't for fashion - though in New York City it would have been in place. It was for ... focusing energy. Just like a satellite dish is designed to send and receive energy waves with a precision of clarity, 'design' - when it serves energy - has *everything to do with channeling Light.* I was becoming a Receiver. And a Sender. Like a lighthouse. I was becoming an energy beacon.

As I walked the streets of New York City, in this vision, I was alone. I saw no 'people'. It was as if they were invisible to me - or I to them.

I noticed … it was my *hands* that radiated Light, not my eyes, or my voice, my heart, or my smile. I walked the streets with my palms open, at a precise angle, glowing, streaming, emanating, casting Light in all directions like the glow of two enormous lighthouse lamps. I was 'lighting the city, with my hands'.

♥

There were visions. And there were very tangible, in my body experiences, too. Like cycling over the Lions Gate Bridge.

Until recently, when the sidewalks were widened as walking and cycle paths, cycling across the Lions Gate Bridge was a daring thing to do. Very few people had the courage or the desire to cross it in this way.

There was a phase during the 'acceleration' when my courage was being tried. I was being 'dared', in a sense, to look at my bodily fears and to ascertain which were real and valid, and which were culturally domesticated. Whew. The only way to sort them was to face them.

I was cycling across the very narrow sidewalk on the bridge, at the prompting of my 'courage' guide. When he / she / it said,

"Take your hands off." What?!? "Take your hands off." There was no ambiguity to its meaning. Hands off the handlebars was all this could mean. Gulp.

There comes a time, in anyone's awakening, when the illusions of the physical must be separated from the real of the beyond.

I lifted my hands, directly upward, a few inches above the handlebars.

It is difficult to describe - something easily understood by anyone who remembers the first moment of realizing that 'Dad' isn't holding the seat of the bicycle, behind you. Or when you ride the surf, free and strong for the first time. Unless you experience this or something akin to it, there aren't sufficient words to convey it.

My guides became my father in that moment. My guides were teaching me how to release fear which had no purpose. It was exhilarating. I can understand why some people are drawn to rock climbing, and free diving, and hang gliding. There is a relying purely on self and spirit in such activities. A *meeting of spirits.*

♥

I lay in bed one morning and realized that I was not 'alone'. I was being visited.

I had participated in an eight week series of Psychic Awareness classes once, and I discovered two things which surprised and intrigued me. One was that - meditation and altered states of awareness seemed so easy for me to access. I could experience whatever was being taught, simply at the suggestion of it. The other surprising discovery was that - I assumed that this was normal. That everyone was like me. I discovered that this wasn't so. The other people around me struggled, with such desire, to 'find' what the teacher was teaching. It seemed as if they were energetically constipated - wanting and reaching and struggling to 'remember'.

One of the things which we were taught in that series of classes was how to meet our spirit guides. Again, I assumed that everyone would have ease with this - because I did.

So the morning I lay in bed realizing I was not 'alone' was not a surprise. I knew what was taking place - in principle! Though I had never experienced precisely this, before.

I tuned in. With eyes closed, I became still and silent inside. Without desire, I simply 'watched'.

A beatific, luminous face shone in my awareness. 'Up' - up and to my left. It was a smiling, white bearded man. There was such a brilliant radiance about him, as if his whole being was a Smile. Even though all I could see was his face - *his entire being shone.* He beamed Light. He *was* Light. Brilliant, glowing, luminous Light.

The Light which he was was a transmission of Love like I'd never experienced before. It was all encompassing, whole, complete. There was nothing about him that was not Light, Love. He was pure, radiating Love.

I felt his Light, his Love wash through me. I was humbled by the beauty and the simple power of it. His whole being was a smile. His entire being smiled toward me.

Then I noticed him telling me his name. 'Og-Mora'. Og-Mora. It suited him so perfectly. Og-Mora.

A few moments of stillness passed - for me to linger in the experience of Og-Mora and his smile, his radiant Love Light.

Then I became aware of a second guide ... introducing herself. She was in front of me and beneath Og-Mora, to my right. She was a delicate, gentle maiden. Strong, yet with no force. She was pure, bright, clear. I felt my own femininity for the very first time. My *true* femininity. Not the conditioned kind.

'Sephaela'. Her name ... was Sephaela.

Again, a brief moment of stillness allowed me to receive her into my full awareness.

Then a third, youthful, strong, powerful, clear male guide appeared. Level with Sephaela, to my left. 'Augustine'. Augustine.

A radiant golden Light power, he was. Like I can imagine Atlas to be. So pure. So strong and benevolent and pure.

A brief moment, again, then the fourth guide in what apparently was a quadrant appeared. Level with Og-Mora, up, to my right. She was more somber, more serious. The least approachable and joyous and friendly of the four, as if she carried a challenging responsibility. As if she was 'at work'. 'Raphael'. She was the Mother. She was ... Raphael.

I was in the presence of four beings - the most benevolent 'people' I had ever met in this lifetime.[6] I felt their presence as my friends, companions on this spirit path.

I didn't know what their purpose was - if there was a purpose, other than to introduce me to beings beyond form. (I still didn't know the 'name' of the entity who had masterminded my healing and my solo tour - just a sense of him, and where he was in relation to me.[7])

Og-Mora, Sephaela, Augustine, and Raphael were 'interim' guides. They were bridges. They were my first experience of

---

[6] Og-Mora explained that they were consciousnesses beyond form. For me to 'see' them, they projected an image of themselves, a holograph-like pattern of Light particles which my inner vision could perceive. Through this image, I could sensitize myself to 'know' them, to recognize and remember them as *essence*. Essence is the energy - core energy - which bridges the seen and the unseen frequencies of existence. Like an amphibian, essence exists equally intact in both 'environments'.

[7] Each guide was oriented in physical space 'in relation to me'. This was instrumental in my noticing their presence, recognizing them precisely, and receiving their message.

disincarnate beings. Of angels. They helped me through the acceleration phase. They 'lifted me higher', such that eventually I could meet guides of even higher vibrations. For the period of time they were with me, they were heart warming friends.

♥

I had a similar, yet more 'serious' experience another morning. I was lying in bed, fresh from waking, when I became aware ... that I was being 'protected'. As I lay in stillness, attuning to what was taking place ... I began to sense them. Two enormous hands, radiating bright golden yellow Light.[8] They were ... in the 'C' curves on either side of my neck, above my shoulders, beneath my head. These two enormous hands were facing directly forward, emphatically beaming this golden yellow Light out, beyond me.

They were like guards, like sentinels. They were protecting me.

A wave of ... concern washed over me. Until this point in my acceleration there had been no fear, no sense of danger whatsoever. It all felt innocent - intriguing and awe-inspiring, yet completely innocent.

---

[8] *Light* is distinct from Earthly 'light' as we know it. *Light* is a luminous *glow* which radiates beyond the 'physics' of this physical world ... For instance the auric glow around celestial bodies and above the crowns of saints and angels as

Why was I now being 'protected'? I asked this question into space. No answer came. Yet I felt a subtle reassurance. A reassurance that *because* this protection was in place now, I would be fine. Though no guidance was directly telling me this, I knew that I was being led into territory that I'd never been in before. Territory of the psychic 'war'.

♥

A message I'd received, on the hike down from Garibaldi Lake, kept repeating itself. Accelerating down the path, with full packsack on my back, I had several times caught a fleeting glimpse out to my side of a beautiful waterfall.

My automatic response would have been to stop, and to walk back. To take a moment to enjoy this glorious view.

Not now. This 'voice' … gentle yet emphatic, as if I was not to argue with it, said, "Don't look back."

I knew it didn't just mean … 'now'. 'This' moment. It was utilizing this moment, and my love for nature, as an example to teach me. To let go. To *let go entirely of the past.*

"Don't look back."

---

often depicted in paintings. It is a lustrous, soul enriching radiance emanating from an unseen Source.

Be in the present, fully free with all of my energy to move forward.

'Don't look back.'

♥

I was also given this simple message, a message to share with others, with anyone who asked for deeper information about my experiences.

"Open yourself to possibility." And ... "Get your house in order."

Intriguingly, the people who asked were always able to sense the cryptic message encoded in the 'obvious' of these words. The deeper meaning. The real, intended communication.

Open your mind to perception beyond the limitations of what society believes is 'real'. Open your mind to *energy*. Let it reveal to you ... a far more infinite reality.

And ... take care of your unfinished business. 'Lighten your load.' Bring old grudges to peace. Sort through your belongings. Let go of attachments.

'While in form, free yourself from your *perceptual dependence on form.*'

Dissolve your fear of the 'unknown'.

Get your house in order. And open yourself to possibility. Two directives. Simple. And huge.

♥

I'd hardly read since I was in high school. I'd loved reading then, and writing theses and essays. Yet, since school, I always seemed somehow dissuaded from reading. I couldn't sit still, with a book, not doing something else as well! Somehow I couldn't justify reading. And ... when I did try to delve into a book, nothing held me. They all seemed so shallow. Void of the spiritual food I needed to eat.

So I didn't read.[9]

During this acceleration phase though, this changed. Three books came to me, and I feasted on them.

One was a hand published book which traveled via the grapevine, being passed from one person to the next. A Gathering of Eagles. It was the personal story of a man who had been 'led out on a limb', being guided to travel the world in trust that his needs

---

[9] Later, my guides explained to me that this had been intended. That, in not studying creation and evolution theories, and religious and political ideologies, I was free to enter 'seclusion' with a 'virgin mind'. This would make my awakening easier - as there wouldn't be other theories and ideals for my awakening visions to debate. And it would make my awakening more challenging - for in the 'void' of reading and learning and adopting other people's beliefs, mine, for a time, would stand in me, alone.

would be met. This simple book told a tale of synchronicity - of trusting in the moment. 'Letting the moment - and spirit - lead.'

Another was a book about angels. I read it voraciously. One night, after reading into the evening hours, I had a dream. In it, I saw precise details. The 'where', the 'what', the 'how'. It was a 'laughter clinic' that I was to open, at 4th and Arbutus in Vancouver. There were balloons everywhere. And people laughing from their bellies in every room. It was a place of healing through release into laughter.

I awoke the next morning, with clear details of the dream still vivid in my mind. Though it intrigued me, I sensed that this dream was a 'stretching' dream. Opening me to possibility. It wasn't solid, in the sense of a certainty that it would take place 'in form'. It was more like … an asking. Just as the guide over my left shoulder had asked me to 'let go control'. It was an asking - asking if I would. If I would be willing to build it, to trust it, to bring this 'vision' into manifest form.

A third book which tore open my former life was Star-Borne: A Remembrance for the Awakened Ones. I had never read a book like this before. It was completely channeled - in 'code', like the book I was about to write (though I didn't know this yet!). It fed me in a way a book never had before. It fed my *soul*.

Just as Solara, the writer, said in her foreword, it triggered memory in me. Deep soul memory. Her writing was simply a 'prompt'. A prompt for me to awaken from the life dream ... and remember.

One of the chapters was on recognizing your cosmic name. And yet again, the mere suggestion was like a laxative, the experience gliding into my being without further help. I lay in trance, a state of consciousness which, in the months and years to come, I would recognize and welcome from a place so deep inside me.

In this mild trance, unaware of the stimuli of the physical world and attuned to the wisdom of within and beyond ... I began to 'know'. To remember. To recognize. My energy name.

Anaqua. Borealis.

I flinched. I drew back. It was too 'hot' for me. How could I, Ariole, this young woman in flesh, live up to the potency of that name? How could I ... be it?

I listened in, as if an observer, unattached, to the 'meaning' of this name.

An, the centre star in Orion's belt. The star through which all energy of creation 'flew'. (More on this later.)

Aqua, the liquid light.[10]

Bo, the moment of explosion[11], when energy passed through An into what became creation.

---

[10] The energy of white gold Light.

[11] The energy of silver blue Light. Together, the white gold and the silver blue *unify duality.* They anchor - they become - the *white Light.*

Realis, form. Here. Real. Now.

Anaqua Borealis. The moment, of consciousness coming into Time, into form.

The next few months of my life would embody my awakening into this role. Awakening to what it means. To what - ultimately - it *is*. The fledgling stages ... of my Earthly initiation.[12]

Not knowing this was to come, and feeling 'Anaqua Borealis' to be too 'hot' for me to 'accept' ... I was given ease, relief, a sense that ... to think of myself as 'Anaqua Realis' would be, for now, enough.

♥

We are living in an amazing time. I could feel this - something that I'd never noticed before. It was palpable. I could feel it in my cells.

I sensed that this may be the first time in history that humans have had the opportunity to *be conscious of their evolution.* That, as a species, we have never had the ability before to observe our own awakening.

---

[12] Each of us has a very precise role to play in the awakening of humanity. We each are a very unique piece of this 'puzzle'. Like the Kayapo Indians of the Amazon, each of us holds a skill, a role, a *knowing* unique to the thrival - the ultimate awakening - of the 'tribe'.

♥

In the bathroom, standing, beside the window. And I could feel it … that my attention was being drawn, out. Out towards a star, a star which I could feel yet could not see.

And with this came the assuring 'sense'. That no matter where I 'go', physically, on this Earth. If I tune in, and link up. I am connected. I am always connected. By a strand of invisible numinous intelligence. I am connected, like an umbilical cord, to this star.

♥

Walking across a street, midway across the pedestrian crossing, it came to me. It pierced into my awareness, like two worlds meeting, in the *moment of that step.*

'I would not have a funeral.'

It seemed like the most normal realization. Real, and true.

Yet I recognized there was something 'odd' about this. Something 'not the norm'.

I continued to observe this piercing vision as I walked.

I saw that my 'body' would 'vanish'. There would be no trace of it.   No body, and thus no funeral.   I would, energetically, 'vanish'.[13]

It was like realizing something that I'd always known.

I recognized the unusualness of this awareness, in western human terms. And yet it felt so true and 'normal', now, to me.

♥

Sitting in one of the Psychic Awareness classes. The teacher is leading us ... somewhere. And I am ... *flying!*

I watch, my awareness perceiving itself in my body and as a witness outside of it, both at the same time.

Body relaxed, sitting in the chair, legs releasing towards the ground ... my 'light body' rises up. Up. Floating. Up.

It planes, horizontal to the ground, as if above a field of golden wheat.

---

[13] Some time later I would come to remember the distinction between death and ascension. This was a flash of memory - a pre-cognition - of ascension.

In death, we leave the energy of the body 'behind'. In ascension, we take it with us. That is, in death our 'soul' (our awakened Mind - our consciousness) arises to the 'soul plane', yet it is still caught by the 'ceiling' which locks us into the Wheel of Time - a continuous experience of Space, incarnate life, and Time. In ascension, we leave the Wheel of Time. We evolve beyond its frequency. We return to an illumined state of consciousness - of Being - beyond limitation.

And then it flips … and spins … and darts! And stops on a dime. And shoots off at an amazing velocity, with no acceleration in 'Time'.

I watch, and sense, and feel, amazed.

Then I realize … this is what we used to do! I am merely remembering, in my body - my light body - and my mind … what we used to be able to do!

We are gradually re-evolving. Reclaiming, regaining *abilities that we have forgotten.*

♥

These one-of-a-kind experiences - the 'accelerated awakening' of the past two months - had meticulously, ingeniously, swiftly set me up. It was like a very rapid - invisible to the outside observer - maturation process. Spiritual and psychic maturation.

I was beginning to get a sense … that I was to write a book. In fact, one morning, the book began to write itself.

I lay in bed, fresh from waking (a place and a body position which was to become so familiar to me), and I felt a 'nudge' inside. I knew I was to get up briefly, and collect pen and paper. Which I did.

Lying down again, propped on my left elbow, it began to flow. I didn't 'think'. It wrote.

A whole chapter, complete without editing, wrote itself through me. I was the scribe.

When it subsided, complete and cognizant of this, an 'Outline' was written. My hand held the pen, and touched it to the page. The rest took place without my effort or my intention.

The Outline complete, 'I' was free to observe and to reflect again.

Something miraculous had just occurred. And yet ... it was a process familiar to me ... through my younger experiences of scribing poetry. And ... through my magical experience of the 'left shoulder guide' who had so eloquently dictated to me the details of my solo tour.

So I wasn't alarmed, or wowed. I simply realized that I had agreed to this. On some level, I had agreed. And now - 'here in the flesh' - I was agreeing, again.[14] It was benign. I had been made available. I was obviously to be its scribe.

What I noticed, when I reflected on the 'Outline', was that ... the map of the book was crystal clear. Up to a point. I could sense that the last two chapters were 'missing'. When I queried this, I was given a clear, tangible, embodied sense that ... they would be known to me, *just in time to write them.*

---

[14] The Higher Self gives the 'green light' - it volunteers - it oversees our timing, our development, our safety. And on our higher levels of consciousness it agrees to a process of 'life' being set into motion. The lower self - or 'I' - must then agree again. This is the process of spirit being manifested into form.

This felt like a bit of a mystery.

I could accept that, intrigued as I was, as several times before in my life I had experienced an awareness that 'it' knew ... whatever 'it' was!!!!

So I accepted this mystery. And I accepted that somehow 'I' was about to give birth to it.

I noticed something else. Without my having 'crafted' it - or ever having consciously thought that 'I' would write a book ... this book, it clearly knew what it was about. Its topic ... was 'healing'.

♥

Dedicated to the writing of this mysterious book, I acknowledged my willingness to be its 'secretary'.

I presumed, as the writing had begun so easily and fluidly while in my home, that the entirety of this book would be written there.

I had a strong sense that, at this particular juncture of writing - in the wee stages of birthing this book - I was to visit my friend Ron, in Seattle. I called him up. He was eager to have me visit.

To make a medium length story short, it was while I was in Ron's home that I felt - evidently I was! - safe enough to see the 'vision'. Or more aptly, my 'mission'. While I was in Ron's home, I saw the place of my seclusion. *The manifestation. Of the vision when I was ten.*

Like cosmic gears shifting into place, the miraculous (and largely unseen) orchestration of my life had 'clicked'. The stepping stones had led me to the Now.

I returned to Vancouver. Three or four undeniable synchronicities rapidly constellated to solidify my knowing.

The aunt of a good friend of mine was going away for six weeks. Could I house-sit for her? In her *cedar log cottage.*

It was at Shuswap Lake. 'Blind Bay' to be precise.

A powerful healer and seer friend whom I'd recently met, Lars, was speaking that very night. In Shuswap Room.

And Lars (though he didn't remember ever saying this, when I asked him later) said to me imploringly, as if a command. "Take care of yourself, Ariole. Go straight to Source. No middle men."

Go straight to Source.

Lars also urged me … not to tell anyone where I was going. For thought can intrude as strongly as form. And what I was going to do in this cedar cottage of my 'vision', I needed to have no intrusion for.

That evening, I tied my sleeping bag onto the carrier of my bike, and I cycled to a grassy knoll overlooking the sea at Jericho Beach. The sleeping bag was to keep me warm as I lay beneath the stars, soothed by the lull of the sea.

I lay there, not to determine if I was to go into seclusion. I lay there, to come to terms with it.

The vision I'd had when I was ten - and its two repetitions, gently reminding me of it, over the years - had prepared me for this. Though I didn't understand it, really, at all - I knew I was to do it. There was no fear. Just a recognition that I was entering something which 'I' had no physical map for. - Though evidently, 'someone else' (disincarnate), did.

I truly was being led.

I wrote a letter - to my grandmother - as a letter to my family. It said, 'Don't worry about me. I've done one-of-a-kind initiatives before. I'll be fine. I'll be away for awhile. I will contact you again … though I don't know when.'

It was quite a cryptic note, though it was as honest as I could be. I didn't know exactly why I was going - except to write 'the book'. I didn't know exactly where I was going - except to the 'log cabin, in the woods'. I didn't know exactly what I was writing - except that it was 'about healing'.

And I didn't know when 'I' would be back.

Enter Seclusion

I must admit I felt resistant to going. - Not to fulfilling the vision, and its quest. Just to being away from people for so long. It had been only months since I completed my inaugural solo tour. And that had been the most isolating experience of my life. I had longed, by the end of that tour, to 'come off stage'. To be very engaged in society, very social. Perhaps to 'compensate' for having felt so isolated. The stress of being onstage alone had been intense.

So this, now - being asked to leave everyone behind at *the* time in my life when I felt, so strongly inside myself, that I wanted *more* people contact - this was the biggest price I could be asked to pay.

So I bargained (or so I thought)! I said to 'the wind' - to whoever or whatever was guiding me, here. I will write so hard. I will work so fast. That I'll be done writing this book and be out of seclusion in six weeks, max.

That was my commitment to myself.

How things change, when you're swept.

♥

All I had in terms of 'tangible anchors' going into seclusion, was a message that … "Field of Dreams - the movie - it's your script". A voice, from somewhere, assuring me that … 'I had a script'.

I had watched "Field of Dreams". So I knew that it was a story about trust. Trust in voices, in visions, in invisible intelligence. And I knew that Ray Kinsella, the lead character, had faith. Tremendous faith. And that his faith and his courage were tested - and strengthened - as his story evolved.

I was given a strong inner feeling that *his* story - his script - would give me solace as my own unfolded. Yes, in this realm of invisible wonders, having a script in hand would give me tremendous comfort.

And it did.

♥

I arrived, on a Greyhound bus, with thirteen pieces of luggage. The packing for this adventure was clearly guided, for I would never have felt comfortable traveling - particularly via public transport - with so much luggage. Evidently, for the first part of the 'writing', I was to have talismans - energetic anchors or 'symbols' - for each of the phases I was about to write about. Once these talismans were transferred into writing, the 'objects' would be released.

So it came to pass that my luggage quantumly diminished as the writing progressed. Yet, to enter this seclusion, thirteen bags were packed.

I was met at Blind Bay village by Beth, the woman whose cottage I was to house-sit. Beth assisted me to stock up on supplies, as I would have no means of transport other than by foot in the weeks to come.

We arrived at the cottage, she showed me the important details to take care of, and she went about her own packing. When I awoke in the morning, she was gone.

In my first night at the cottage, I had one of the most violent, frightening nightmares of my life. In the dream, I was locked in the basement of a house with two other people. All of the windows were boarded over, so that it was completely black inside. No light shone in.

These two people were heroin junkies, and it was clear that 'H' possessed them in a demonic way.

I was the observer. And observing this terrified me.

I awoke. All was still. The wind blew eloquently through the trees outside. Birds sang, full of delight. Clearly they had not shared this dream.

I was alone. There was no one to speak to. Seclusion had begun.

♥

The first day and a half was spent setting up the energy field of the cottage. I - though I still didn't know by whom (for Og-Mora and the other angels were not within my communication here) - was being meticulously guided. As if, in setting up the cottage, I was being trained. Precisely trained. In how to receive minute details. Through the transmission and reception of *energy*.

Anyone watching this would have thought I was nuts. The whole cottage, in its interior, became a shrine. To what, I did not yet know. I just knew, with no more proof required, that I was being guided, for some reason, to do this. My physical environment was being set up to support what was to unfold in my psychic environment.

And this it did, very well.

Everything was colours. All of the clothing I had brought with me, and the 'objects', were vivid and vibrant hues of light. I was guided what to place where, and how, so that the entire inner cottage became a sanctuary, of Light.[1]

If any of the objects were moved to create 'straight lines', I felt jarred inside. Like a mild electrocution.

Little did I know then, that I was being set up for this. Now. Creating this cottage as a 'receptor'. Like an enormous satellite dish. So that I, the tiny one within it, could hear, crystal clear.

♥

A day and a half later, the cottage was set. I still didn't know who was guiding me, yet it was clear to me that 'I' was not alone.

I felt a brooding unease, a fear. It wasn't a fear of physical danger - of other humans intruding. It was a fear ... of something psychic.

I began to perceive what I can only describe as noxious fumes, sickly yellow green, arising from 'the basement'. I was beginning to sense that I was entering a realm of consciousness thick

[1] I had been attuned to the 'placement of things' in my home for years. Often I 'felt' inside of me what colours and shapes to hang where on the walls, how to balance the environment with plants and, more precisely, on what *angles* to place furniture.

When I did this, I could *feel*, palpably, energy flowing and arcing and spiraling through the space as if the precise placement of 'things' directed the flow - or obstruction - *of energy*. When I was attuned, it felt as if the articulate placement of 'objects' created channels, streams of energy, a vortex of *peace*.

Years later I came across Feng Shui and realized that I had intuitively been practicing one of three of its ancient 'schools'.

with metaphor. I understood, innately, that much of what I was about to experience would be in a language of *symbols*. That I would be able to discern between what was really happening in the physical, and what, in the physical, was a 'symbol'. A teaching. A way for the physical to reveal to me something much deeper. Just like the Native Americans receive messages and teachings from other creatures, symbols would begin, thickly, to evoke this learning and awakening for me.

So 'the basement', I knew, was a metaphor. It *represented* something. It represented that which is underneath. Ultimately, the seed. Immediately, 'rotten illusion'.

Still not knowing who was guiding me, the 'guide(s)' calmed me, sensing my very real fear in the presence of this 'metaphoric' danger.

It was explained to me that there was a war going on over me. The dark forces were doing everything they could to thwart my being in seclusion. For they recognized that the reason I had been led here was to quantumly wake up. And that in waking up, I would create a massive wake, like a tidal wave, stirring many others from their slumber. And this ... would loosen their hold.

This ... was the threat to them, the 'dark forces'. For as people awaken and see through illusion, the dark forces are no longer fed. They can no longer control.

My 'guides' assured me that - I needed to be aware of this tug for my attention. Yet I was safe. They further explained that the dark forces were trying to get me to 'swing'. To collude with them. To serve them.

Yet both I and my guides knew that there was no chance of this. I had been - forever prior to this lifetime, and now - purely committed to serving the Light. To serving consciousness which remembers itself as whole, as 'of God'.

I felt no fear, absolutely no uncertainty about this. I knew within myself that there was not even a slight chance that the dark forces could persuade me.

What I recognized, though, was that they would try. They would try by frightening me, by intimidating me.

My guides then clarified this: No matter how potent the dark forces may appear, in any moment, there is at least 51% Light present. In every moment, the Light is stronger than the Dark.

I realized then, as I would recognize even more clearly in the days ahead, that every moment is a choice point. A choice between the Light and the dark. In every moment, we decide. We decide which of these energy fields to align with.[2]

And in so doing, we become either more dark. Or more *Light*.

---

[2] The Light *remembers*. The dark forgets. Memory as I speak of it here is the only ultimate memory - the memory of our awakened state.

My guides, in empathy of my circumstance, gave me a somewhat physical way to feel safe. It was still energetic, yet more 'in my own language'. I called Ron. It was the second to last time I would speak with him, or with anyone else in the flesh, for months.

I asked him if I could envisage him - hundreds of him, in fact. I would see him, facing outward from the cabin, about a hundred feet away. Hundreds of him would stand, side to side, encircling the cabin, facing outward. He would be my 'guard'.

He said 'Yes'.

I put this into place, energetically, in my mind. And I felt safe.

From then on I could feel the tug of the dark forces, and yet they became weaker and weaker, like a voice becoming more and more distant.

♥

Once the cottage was set, and I had become aware of the battle over me, and I had been put to ease about this - the writing began.

I would wake in the morning, before sunrise. The pads of paper and pens would already be set on the floor beside my bed. I would reach down for them, prop myself on my left elbow, and begin to write.

The sun would rise. I would continue writing. I would feel hunger pangs. I would continue writing. I would feel thirst, or a need to pee. And I would continue writing. My physical 'needs' disappeared. All that was, was the writing.

After what I finally calculated to be about seven hours, the writing would 'complete itself'. It would come to a point of 'closure' for the day.

I would lay back on the bed, and swiftly fall asleep. In my sleep, which bridged into waking, I would be shown things. The 'teachings' had begun. I would be shown patterns of energy, and be trained to understand their meaning. Often these were abstract, yet their *meaning* would be crystal clear to me. In this trance state, much of the teaching could remain abstract.

I would 'come to', returning to relatively 'normal', lucid consciousness, assuming that the day's work was done and that 'I' could now be free to nurture myself and to have some 'fun'. Immediately, like clockwork, every day, the 'outline' for the next day's writing would spill. In point form, the anchors for the next day's writing would be written down.

Again, I would feel released, as if the work (or this phase of it) was complete. I would get up from bed, for the first time that day. I would, without thinking about it, carry with me yet another stack of pads of paper and pens. And I would make my way to the living room. Here, I would promptly lie. On the sofa. It felt refreshing, to be in another room with vaulted ceilings, much more light, and a view up to the loft above.

In a somewhat daze, I would watch wafts of awarenesses breeze through my mind. This phase of the day was the time for 'gratitude'. I would write thanks to all of the people and places which had paved the way for this. I would feel overwhelming awe at the experience I was now in - a gratitude in the depth of my being for having been asked to do this, here, now. For I knew that, in some way, what I was experiencing was 'rare'. Many times I felt humble to a power I cannot describe. It was like I was in the presence of a God.

After some hours in the living room, I would truly be released to care for my physical self. I would go to the kitchen, and prepare food.

My appetite was fading, and so I ate very little. It felt less and less important to eat 'food'. For I was, more and more, being fed *life force.*[3]

♥

This writing went on for two and a half weeks. The very same pattern, every day.

---

[3] Pure energy, that which the Taoists refer to as 'chi', the Yogis as 'prana'.

Each day I was awed by what was being written, and how. I began to 'recognize' it. It was, on one level, the story of 'my life'. And yet it wasn't. It was as if 'my' life ... was being used simply as a template. In fact, it was explained to me by my guides that ... 'anyone could exchange their details for mine. And in so doing, this 'book' ... it would be a catalyst, to wake them up'.

In other words, mine was a *blueprint 'story'*. A story which, energetically, represented others' lives, too.

The book was being written in an amazing way. It was like parables. Nuggets of deep learning, of profound meaning. Elements of my life 'story' were being selected for *what could be taught, through them* ... Chosen for what, within them - like pearls within oysters - could be revealed.

I was in awe of this writing, for I was not writing it. I was, just like the poem from my youth foretold, a 'scribe'.

"the author thinks i am its feather"

♥

It amazed me how well I had been set up for this. How well I had been prepared. Sometimes, in those late afternoon hours in the living room, I would find myself reflecting back to the events of my life. The apparently unrelated 'events'.

And I could now see, in looking back at them, how they were connected. And how they built one upon the next. And how *economical* they were. How so little had been wasted. How, with each succession, I had been brought closer and closer to readiness to be *here*.

♥

After about a week and a half, I began to feel a 'pressure' building. And with this, I noticed several things.

Firstly, every time I had wanted to go outside, or to open a window, I had been dissuaded from this. Gradually, I came to understand that … *this energy was being contained.* And in successfully containing it, it was building in its potency. In its power to awaken. 'Me'.

I also began to recognize the nature of what, so far, was being written. It was … 'horizontal'. It was parables of healing, and of awakening - of learning - 'here', in this physical realm, here, now.

It was about this lifetime.

As the pressure I was sensing increased, I gradually became able to identify it. It was … 'the universe, wanting to explode, through me'. It was as if … it could barely wait for me to 'set the book up'. To write the horizontal story *so that the vertical story could be told.*

I felt tremendous respect from this 'universe', whoever or whatever these energies were. It was as if they knew that, in order for the 'vertical' story to be written, the horizontal story had to be written first.

And yet, the closer and closer I got to the completion of writing the horizontal, of laying the groundwork, the more and more ready to burst they became.

At this point I began to have some quantum experiences. The day to day process of the writing continued, sprinkled with powerful awareness 'explosions'.

I was lying on the sofa one afternoon, on my right side. My eyes were open.

And I began to see it. The metaphor. And the symbol.

The symbol was the beetle. A scarab.

It was … walking, back and forth. Along the rim of the round wooden table, directly in front of my eyes. Back … and forth.

Then I saw the metaphor. It pierced my awareness. The beetle was showing me this: Sewing. Sewing the seam. Between darkness and Light.

The beetle was … I was? The beetle was showing me *me*. That I am … sewing the seam. The seam. Between darkness and *Light*.

Gradually, gradually, I would mature in my comprehension to understand *what this means*.

♥

It is no coincidence that my birth name initials are SEW.
Or that my birth name means Share-Onnnnn ...[4]

♥

The command. Like a directive. Gentle, yet affirming.
"Take a bath."

I was becoming familiar with these 'directives'. Like firm
requests. They always led to a discovery, even though initially each
one, to my naïve mind, seemed initially odd.

"Take a bath."

I already knew how to discern. This is an ability which
exists in all of us, albeit somewhat latent in many people. The
ability to listen within, and to identify that which is benevolent and
that which is malevolent. In seclusion, this ability was being rapidly
honed.

---

[4] I was given the name 'Sharon' at birth. Share-Onnnnn ... To share endlessly,
like the wake behind a swimming bird. Or the piercing ... the ultimate piercing of
the 'Veil' - that cloud of unconsciousness which dominates our minds. And the
long awaited *piercing* of it ... a domino effect, a run, a 'tear'. Like an echo, a sigh,
a wake heard longlast, resonating throughout Space and Time.

So I knew, as with every one of the directives that I would ultimately receive from my guides, no matter how 'dangerous' they might appear, that I was truly safe in each and every one of them.

Discerning this, I entered the bathroom, and began to run water into the huge crowfoot tub. I stripped off my clothes, and I stepped in.

Some minutes passed ... and it didn't seem evident at all 'why' I was there. Me, water, the tub. Was I just ... to 'take a bath'?

I played for a few moments with a yellow plastic duck, truly at odds with the 'why' of this directive.

Then it began, as swift and clear as these experiences always were.

It was as if ... I was listening to ... a radio. And there was static. The ... wires were being ... tuned. And I was now hearing ... it was like a short wave radio station ... a transmission from ... *very far away.*

As this, and all of the phenomenal experiences which were 'delivered to me by my guides', was so effortless to me, I assumed that what I was hearing could be heard by everyone.

I listened. It was 'the news'. Just like an announcer, his voice piercing through the static, his message being heard. "The war is over."

And with that, the transmission ended.

I was 'released', from the bath. As its purpose was over.

I stood up, toweled off, and dressed, unsure precisely what it was that I had just heard.

I walked into the kitchen and, holding a glass of water in my hand, stood facing the window. When I began to hear it. It was *so loud.* Like New Year's Eve, and everyone leaning out of their windows, with noise makers and horns. *Celebrating!*

I assumed that it was all around me - in the 'world', outside. Then ... I realized ... I could *feel* it. 'Up' ... 'above me'! *It was in the galaxies. It was our 'Festival of Friends'.*[5]

They were celebrating! Our freedom from the war! They were celebrating - the imminence of our coming Home!!

I felt them, my long forgotten 'spirit' friends. The thousands of spirits I'd left behind when I 'incarnated' this time. They were still there. All of them (except those who'd incarnated, too). And they were greeting us. Jubilant that, soon 'Time' would be done. And the purpose of 'form' would be complete. And we would be united, again.

I assumed, in my innocence - for I had, all my life, believed that I am no different than any other, that we all have the same inherent gifts and abilities - that if I could hear this 'news', then everyone else on this planet Earth could hear it too.

---

[5] Bruce Cockburn, a gifted and prophetic Canadian songwriter, sings of our 'Festival of Friends'.

I made my way to the living room, sure that I'd see striking changes in the world outside. There was no evidence of it. No evidence of the 'news'.

I called Ron, the last time I would speak with him. I cracked a joke! Something about 'the news', in 'code'! He didn't get it. *Ron* ... didn't get it.

And then I knew. If Ron didn't hear the news ... then who else did? Was I the only one? Or one of a very few?

Somewhat shocked by this, and feeling a tad alone, my guides slowly, ever so gently began to give me a sense of understanding.

They explained that, just like a star 'dying' and its light taking thousands of years to reach our sight, energy on other vibratory levels does this, too. Yes, the war *was over.* I had been led to hear this news. *It was true.* Yet it would take some 'Time' for the effects of this to reach the Earth.

I was, evidently, being attuned to what was taking place on the higher energy levels, 'ahead of our Time'.

This would be the first of several such 'prophecies' I would be shown.

♥

I felt more and more that I was on a 'mission' - a mission that I couldn't yet comprehend. And I felt humbled, and awed, by my increasing awareness of its enormity. And little by little I realized that, for some reason, I had been chosen. And for this - for the opportunity of this amazing experience, here as a human, I felt a depth of gratitude which, to the as yet 'unidentified guides', I frequently expressed.

♥

There were several other profound experiences in those first few weeks.

Often at night, I was led to a window. And through it, to see … a very precise constellation of stars. I immediately recognized it. As a child, under the night sky, my head would involuntarily swing back and up for me to see it. As if I was magnetically drawn to it. Orion's Belt.

Now, I was being led to see it. To truly *see* it. As if studying it. As if *remembering* it. Three stars. Almost equidistant. In a balance.

And the centre star. The *centre* star. Of El An Ra.

Is An.

In soon time it would be explained to me the significance of El and Ra and, even more importantly, of An.

♥

I was also taken, several times, to look out the window at a cluster of three trees.   Three.   There was something highly significant in this. Like I was being 'wired' to recognize the essential importance of 'three'.[6]

For now, I was being taught how to 'align'.

I had had several experiences somewhat like this, during the acceleration period prior to seclusion. I had been led to the base of an old growth 'grandparent' tree, hundreds of years old, in the Carmannah Valley. And I had felt a circuit of energy begin to flow between us.   As if we were 'dialoguing', from our 'unconscious minds'. It felt like the tree and I were downloading archaic wisdom to each other. It was a profound, very tangible experience.

Another time during that period, Sue and I both felt an inner prompting to speak with the whales.   It, too, was a profound experience, one of receiving and transmitting wisdom from the body, particularly from the belly. I noticed - I could feel - that the belly was the 'loudest' region of energy communication, the 'hot spot', the core.

---

[6] Several years later, when I received the 'Second Installment of the Vision', I was brought into memory of Triads, and Trilogies, and Triad Trilogies. More on this later.

That time, there were some words. "What took you so long?" The impatient question of the whale - impatient yet grateful that we were finally there, open, and able and willing to listen.

I had always sensed that whales are more conscious than most humans. That they 'know' things that we are still asleep to.

Humans of the western world so swiftly to assume that other sentient beings are less intelligent than we are. How is it that we measure intelligence? Are we so sure that there is no intelligence that eludes us?

♥

With the three 'wise trees', I was given a clear understanding that I was to 'align with them'. This meant - to align my chakras with theirs.

Trees, as all living things, have chakras - embodied energy centres. The chakras are receiving and transmitting centres (amongst other functions).

In aligning my chakras with those of the three 'wise trees', I became able to communicate with them, still, silent on a level of language which I had forgotten.

Whenever I became aware of communication taking place between me and a creature or an element of nature - as with these three trees - I noticed that it was my *body* communicating, energetically, not my 'mind'. My mind was the witness, the observer.

I was told by my guides that one day, I would teach other humans how to align. I was therefore to pay close attention to how I did it. So that I could convey this clearly, to remind others how, too.

When we align, we 'plug in'. So in aligning my energy centres with An, I was plugging myself into the wisdom of An. Aligning with these trees, I was plugging in to the wisdom, the memory, which these trees held and which they metaphorically represent.

♥

One afternoon, standing in the kitchen, facing out through the window, I was opened to a perception of the world's pain.

My nervous system was strained like wires pulled taught. I could hear the screaming of the trees. The screaming from within the Earth itself.

And then I realized. It was humans' pain more than anything that I was being tuned in to.

I realized then, that the Earth is waiting. Patiently waiting. For humans to release their pain. That the Earth can take all of humanity's pain, and transmute it. That if humans were to release their pain, cleanly, and allow Earth to carry it and to transform it, she would. Like a river, she would dissolve it, she would transport it away from our experience. She would cleanse us.

She is fully capable of this. In fact, humans' pure expression of their pain cannot harm her. It is their withholding of their pain that can. And does.

I had a sense, that if … for only five minutes … humans were to cleanly release their pain. To release the puss from their emotional wounds - like the releasing of pressure during the eruption of a volcano. If, for only five minutes, humanity were to do this … *What a different world this would be!!* Only *five minutes* - of all of humanity draining pressure from its pain - would completely transform the nature of human existence.

And it would completely alter the relationship of humans with Earth, our temporary home.

I could only handle the intensity of perceiving this pain for what felt like thirty seconds. My guides were well aware of this. For then my nervous system was set immediately at ease. The volume of the pain dissipated. My awareness of it dissolved.

But my memory of it never would. I had heard it, seen it, felt it. Now I knew it was there.

♥

In all of these experiences I felt that I was, gradually, being initiated. Into a wisdom which I faintly remembered.

I knew that, in our current western culture, we had no reference for understanding or valuing initiations. So although this seclusion experience was profoundly real and I could sense the enormity and vital relevance of it to our Time, I knew that very few of my 'countrymen' would have any context in which to comprehend it. In a sense, my boat was being led farther and farther away from the shore.

The Guides Introduce Themselves

No sooner had I completed the 'horizontal writing' than it broke. Like birth waters, an entire new realm of perception opened before me.

My guides began to identify themselves.

It didn't happen immediately. In fact, as soon as the horizontal writing was complete, I found myself lying motionless on the sofa. For two and a half weeks.

It took this long to fine tune my wiring.

I was in trance most of this time, the recipient of a highly delicate operation. Like a high tech surgery.

Trance is akin to a near death experience in many ways. In trance, the bodily functions slow almost completely, acquiescing themselves to a higher level of consciousness. In a sense, the body goes dormant so that the Mind can awaken. Or rather, so that the mind can awaken to the Mind. So that the Soul can re-cognize itself.

I was never frightened by trance. I always felt *relieved* by it. It felt like … the warm womb of primal experience. It felt like … returning to the state of pure spirit before this life.

I had been experiencing involuntary trances for several years. They had been introduced to me gradually so that I could 'recognize them' and not feel frightened by them. For when in trance, the 'logic' of the mind goes to sleep. And the abstract functions fire up. In trance, until a person is well adept, normal human activities are suspended. Higher levels of consciousness open up, becoming accessible, and the person in the trance recognizes - like I imagine a nun would recognize her commitment to God - that this - the state of trance - is the most important 'activity' at the moment. There is a recognition that the 'arrival' of a trance is a gift. It is an opening. Like the lowering of a drawbridge to access a great castle. The drawbridge lowers when it will. It cannot be forced, though it can sometimes be requested. To be invited into the castle is a sacred opportunity.

And so trance becomes recognized as perhaps the most important 'activity' of one's life.

This became the case with me.

I call it 'spontaneous meditation', because it leads me. At no point in my life did I consciously seek it. It sought me.

♥

So there I was, lying on my side, for two and a half weeks.

Interestingly, synchronistically, I had received two visions just prior to entering seclusion. One regarding my hair. And one regarding my tooth.

While still in Vancouver, before journeying to 'Blind Bay', I had a dream. In the dream I saw that my hair had been cut in a very precise style. It was asymmetric. Very clearly the right side was long, soft and completely covering my ear. The left side was short, exposing my ear.

The next morning Lars ubiquitously recommended his new hair stylist to me. I knew there was a connection. I made an appointment, and I sat in this man's chair.

He asked me if there was a particular style that I'd like. A voice in me urged me to simply "trust him". And so I told him nothing of the dream.

He proceeded to tell me of a dream he'd had the night before! Of a bold new haircut. He was 'waiting', he said, for the 'right head to show up'!

I sat in his chair, and I allowed this magical process to unfold. Without saying a word to each other, he *cut my hair exactly as I'd seen it.*

I let this experience pass as just another of the phenomena of my acceleration. Until I was in seclusion, lying on the sofa, being 're-wired'. Here, the vision of 'the haircut' seemed suddenly important. Like it had been *planned*. For ... my right ear was cushioned, by the long silky soft hair. And my left ear was exposed ... to 'hear'.

Also in the weeks prior to entering seclusion, I was shown a vision that I was to have a tooth crowned. A gold crown, specifically. And, even more specifically, on my lower left side.

It was months later that I came across information identifying gold as a 'conductor'. Yet again, my preparation was 'planned'. I had been 'fitted' with a precious tooth whose properties would assist in my subtle 'receiving' of communication through *energy*.

So, for two and a half weeks, I remained motionless. Curled up in fetal position, on my right side. I barely moved. For if I moved, it was as if ... I inadvertently jostled loose a kind of 'delicate wiring'.

In a light state of trance, I was able to perceive beyond the seen. It was as if a subtle, fragile, highly intricate operation was taking place. I was being ... 'released', from my primary wiring of perception, locked into this physical world. And I was being 're-wired', to a much more fine, 'cosmic' frequency. In short, I was being attuned to the 'far out'.

It was no coincidence (more like a 'cosmic joke'!) that I had been led to begin my seclusion in 'Blind Bay'. For the process I was now in was one of being 'gently made blind, in order to see'. I was being guided to let go my attachment to - my belief in - this physical world as being 'it'. As being the totality of reality. And in so doing, I was being opened to *what is beyond this.*

It was a courageous process, in a sense. Though it was made much easier by my being completely removed from the world of human interactions. For beliefs are upheld by humans in community. Community is in a sense the 'glue' which holds world views in place. The primary world view, or paradigm, of the 'civilized' world is that only that which is physical is real. If we journey back in Time or visit current indigenous cultures, we find that the 'dream time' is as real, if not more so, in the community's beliefs and values, than is the so-called 'reality' of the physical world. So, being a 'western white woman', the most successful way for me to be 're-wired' - to become able to perceive that which is beyond form - was to be removed from the glue of the consensus beliefs.

This is why I was brought into 'seclusion'. Why I was to 'contain' the energy of my awakening, by staying inside the intensifying field of memory, of 'Light', within the cottage.

This is why I was to speak with no one else.

For ... what would I say? How could I describe what I was witnessing, what I was awakening to, what I was remembering, what I was perceiving? I had left the mainstream world and its perceptual shore. And yet I was adrift (and would be for several months). I didn't yet have a construct - a 'new world view' which I could articulate to others. A 'new shore'. I didn't yet have a new picture which I could convey in words.

Quite plainly, I was 'between world views'. I was inside a kind of consciousness embryo, a new world view in the making.

Letting go my 'sight' - my perception and understanding of what 'is' - was actually a relief to me. For on a level I must have known that what the western world believes in is incomplete.

I'd never been a member of a religion. My parents left the church when I was young. I'd never followed politics or ideologies - they went in one ear and out the other, without ever making sense or 'sticking' for me.

In fact, as I mentioned earlier, since high school, I hardly read.

So to a large extent, my mind was clear.

This made 'receiving the memories' more direct and straightforward. They were, in some ways, enough of a shock to my system as they were. Without having to wade through and balance and battle against other ideologies I could, quite simply, let them 'land'. I could *perceive them for what they were.*

As seclusion evolved, my guides began to lovingly call me the 'Queen of Courage'. What they were asking me to do required boldness and determination - psychically, psychologically, and physiologically.

I could feel their admiration for me, the one of us in physical form. Some of them had been in form before, others not. They all seemed to recognize and respect the unique challenge of being spirits incarnate. I felt tremendous respect of them to me.

♥

I learned to not move around much in those two and a half weeks. The more I was 'un-wired' from the old neurological wiring, the less 'familiar' consciousness I had to return to. So it quickly became to my advantage to let these 'invisible guides' do their obviously masterful work. The stiller I lay, the more secure I felt. For I could 'feel' the subtle wiring becoming more secure, more 'solid' by the day.

It was like 'I' was the short wave radio. And 'I' was being fitted … to receive stations 'far out'.

♥

One day the foundation of the re-wiring was obviously complete. Because my guides - up to this time intriguingly evident yet 'anonymous'!! - began to identify themselves.

I had never experienced anything even remotely like this. Since this experience, only twice have I felt anything akin to it again.[1]

It was like being introduced to my family. For my guides were, it was clear, a prominent ring in the great ripple of my energy 'family'.

What was presented to me, in the four (?)[2] days that it took for my guides to introduce themselves, was that *together, we spanned four planes of existence.* A very economical design. One of us represented each of these four dimensions.

I'll start with me. I was, of this 'team', the one incarnate, in the flesh. The one in the '3D'.

'Ariole'

---

[1] When I remembered the 'Triad' with Pedro and Alessandro •. And when I remembered the '48 + 2' of the 'Beak'. Both are stories which are to come.

[2] I don't know precisely how long, in 'Earth' Time, it took for my first three tiers of guides to introduce themselves. I've always sensed, since then, that it was 'four days'. The fourth tier of my guides identified itself about a week later, when the first round of 'introductions' had settled and was well integrated and had been welcomed by me.

I was also the female one. It wasn't that the others were 'male'. They 'presented' themselves as male, to 'anchor my femininity'.

It was made very clear to me that guides are not inherently male - or female. In fact, all energy is, at its essence, 'androgynous'. It is, ultimately, a pure balance between the 'yin and the yang'. Between the masculine and the feminine principles.

So, merely because *I was the only one of us in the flesh,* my guides 'appeared' to me as more masculine. The 3D incarnate one balancing the 'Light'-ness of the disincarnates. This 'design' was merely a matter of 'ballast'. I anchored them, and they anchored me.

So I was the 'first tier', the female principle existing primarily (more on this later) in the 'physical'.

My first guide was the *soul* of someone currently incarnate in the physical - not his *conscious* self.

'Allesandro'

My second guide was the soul of a disincarnate being who had once (actually, more than once) been incarnate. He currently existed on the 'soul plane' - the plane 'between incarnations'.

'Shakey'

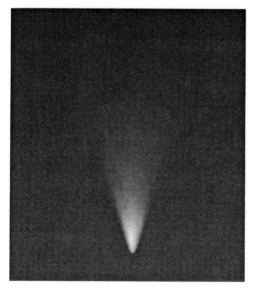

And my third guide had never been incarnate.

'Sourcey'

And as I mentioned in the recent footnote, a fourth guide introduced itself to me about a week later, in 'Hope'!

'Ansy'

Four tiers of consciousness. This was my 'team'.

They introduced themselves and mapped out this 'mobile' - incarnate, soul of incarnate, soul of disincarnate, disincarnate - this 'map' for my easy comprehension. It all took place in what seemed like a very swift time.

**'Ariole with four tiers of guides
energetically anchoring five dimensions of consciousness'**

And as soon as their 'introductions' had been effectively received by me, *they all began to speak at once!*

It was - even though all of this was transpiring purely in my attunement to and thus cognizance of subtle energy, and not in this 'physical space' - it was overwhelming. I felt dumbfounded in the midst of this sudden chaos, as if I had instantly awakened into the hubbub of a marketplace in full mayhem.

In that instant ... my being must have sent out a signal that alerted my guides, even though I didn't realize that I'd sent it! For everything stopped.

And immediately they recognized what was missing. I had felt like a runway overloaded with jets landing. Like an inter-dimensional air traffic controller who had been suddenly swamped.

They knew precisely what to do, and in an instant that felt like a split second, they were already activating their empathic response.

Each one of them determined 'where' - in relation to me - they would speak from. So that initially I could identify them by their 'orientation to me, in space'. As I became more adept in recognizing their essence, their 'subtle energy', I would not need this. But that would be a later, intermediate stage. For now I was an infant in this. I was a beginner.

My first guide was, as I mentioned, the soul or higher self or canopy of consciousness of Alessandro •, a highly awake global activist, musician and writer - a 'musical poet'. Though 'he the man' was not completely awake to and cognitively aware of our connection, his soul very much was. Slightly older than me in 'Earth Time', and much more visible in the world, it was his soul that would guide me. And as 'he, the man' was currently here on Earth, in incarnate flesh, his soul's presence as my guide would give me enormous comfort in the times ahead.

For I was in flesh, awakening. And no matter what my 'disincarnate' guides could grant me in terms of love and compassion and support, this 'thread' - this connection via a guide 'in form' - would give me solace in the most difficult of the times to come.

My second guide was, in fact, the entity who had sat above my left shoulder. The one who had guided me to heal my knee, and to tour solo. This was the 'genius', the mastermind who had dictated all of that miracle's myriad details to me.

Let's call him Shakespeare. The soul, or supermind, of Shakespeare. (Not the personality. The *soul*. There is a similarity, yet a distinct difference, here.)

I called him Shakey.

My third guide was the pure essence of *God*.

And so, in order that I could effortlessly identify who was who[3] in the early stages of seclusion, these guides each 'oriented themselves in space, around me'.[4]

Allesandro was, with a few exceptions in the future, always directly behind me. His energy field was approximately the size of a man. When I tuned into him, here, I was able to begin to identify his essence. He was very gentle, incredibly compassionate, loving and kind. He was ultimately respectful and deeply attuned to the enormity of what I was being guided to do.

---

[3] These guides never projected themselves to me as 'visions'. Rather I 'felt' them, energetically, and I could see them as pools or 'auras of Light'. Each of them, as a 'Light pool', was a specific density, colour, and 'size'. Nor could I 'hear' them, like distinguished human voices. Though I could 'feel' their resonance. *And thus I became able to recognize them through recognizing their frequency of consciousness.*

[4] They are not, in fact, limited to size or to orientation in Space. They exist well beyond that. Like Og-Mora, Sephaela, Augustine and Raphael, they simply emanated an *energy field representation of themselves,* which I then perceived as orientations in Space. For Space is a phenomenon of my (human) mind, not of their (transcended) existence. ("You can't fit a pea into a pinhead.") Omni-dimensional existence cannot be reduced to the consciousness of the human mind. The mind must *open to* it, thus *expanding to reach It.*

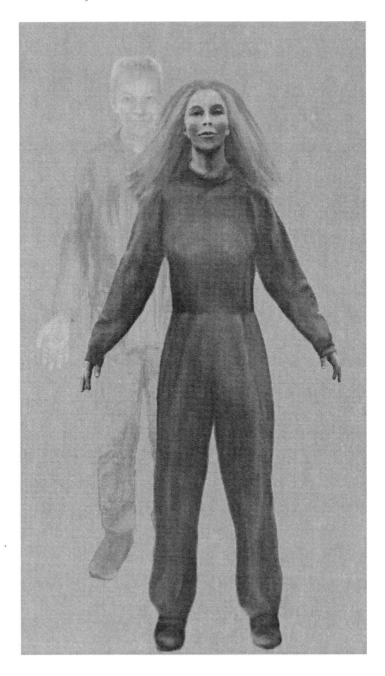

'Ariole with Allesandro's 'soul''

Shakey was, with very rare exception, always about six inches tall, directly over my left shoulder. On exceptional occasions, when I was threatened by psychic attacks, he would instantly, in a split second, inflate himself to 'human size' and stand energetically behind me to protect me. When the danger was gone, he would resume his unassuming place above my left shoulder.

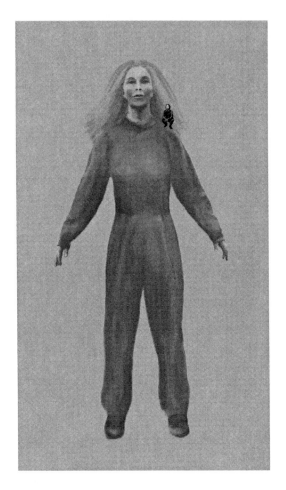

'Ariole with Shakey'

God, or Sourcey as I came to call 'him', always communicated to me from directly in front of me, up, at about a forty-five degree angle, at what felt like four to six feet away. The most pure, still, radiant presence. Quiet, humble in his strength.

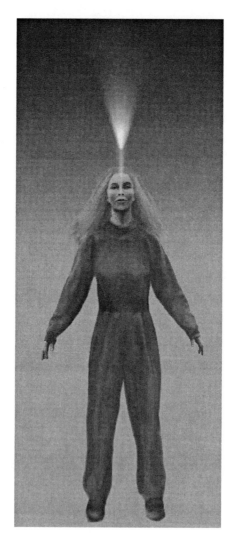

'Ariole with Sourcey'

Alessandro was present yet 'faint' to me for much of the next few weeks of seclusion. He and I would have an 'acquainting' phase later on, during which I would attune more distinctly to his presence.

In this first stage of seclusion, Shakey communicated with me non stop. (More on this in a moment.)

And Sourcey ... his was the most sublime, sweet, pure communication. It felt like ... once every two weeks ... 'he' would ... say a few words. A brief phrase. And the energy, the Light, the radiance of those words would feed me on such a rich level that the 'afterglow' would last two weeks. His communication would emanate through me for a fortnight.

His was such a pure, direct, gentle, source-full communication.[5]

Shakey. He was my 'left hand man'. He was with me constantly, in my wake and in my sleep. One night I awoke from a dream. I was surprised to notice him, sitting with me, watching out for me like a shepherd with his beloved flock.

I asked, 'Shakey, do you not sleep?' Innocent, naïve I was. He explained that, as a spirit, he could always be with me. He had no needs - for sleep, or food, or his own bodily functions. He said that many spirit guides looked out for numerous people. Yet he, at

---

[5] Sourcey's communication was so profound because it wasn't as 'stepped down' as Shakey's or Alessandro's. It was of a higher voltage, a higher 'potency'. Each strata of guides 'stepped down' the energy to the next, keeping it intact and pure, yet less intense.

this phase in Time, was looking out only for me. He was 'assigned', he said jokingly, solely to me.

I felt in a sense that he was my bodyguard. Yet he was so much more than that. In the weeks and months that followed, he became my closest friend. I was well beyond being able to speak with any of my 'human' friends - not until a new, articulate-able world view had gelled that I could express. Until then, it was my guides and me.

I have never felt so un-alone in all my life. Yes, in seclusion I was without human companionship. Yet my guides supported me, and nurtured me, and befriended me in a way that no humans ever had.

♥

Over the course of a couple of days the experience of meeting and being in the presence of known, identifiable guides 'normalized'. It was as if this was the way it had always been. (Amazing how quickly we can adapt!)

Then the deeper teachings began.

Seclusion became what I refer to as the 'First Installment of the Vision' - the laying of the ground. Though much was let go of and much more was remembered, I still didn't have a cohesive structure to my new awarenesses by the end of it. I was, to a large degree, still 'in process' at the end of seclusion - though I wouldn't realize this until the 'Second Installment of the Vision' arrived. This was several years later.

Here in seclusion, it was a potent process of deconstruction and the returning to me of long lost memory. It was a deconstruction of 'illusion'.

Layers of perception were dissolved, making way for profound comprehension and re-accessing of memories. Some of the key principles - memories regained - included these ...

We, here on Earth as humans, are merely a 'shaft' of who we are in totality. As long as we perceive only our physical selves, we perceive only the 'little brother', the 'little sister' of who we are. The 'big brother', the 'big sister' is what we often refer to as our 'higher self'. An aspect of our consciousness which has access to the 'birds' eye view'. An aspect of our consciousness which can perceive the 'flow' - existence beyond the limitation of Space and Time.

When we tap into our higher self, we become more whole. We become more power full - the ultimate in benevolence.

'the shaft'

♥

Each of us houses a personal parallel to the cosmic birth canal, the energetic pathway through which 'creation' was born.

This parallel is our own umbilical cord - *the region of our belly.* Through attunement to our belly, we can awaken to all memory through and prior to Time.

♥

We are, individually and collectively, in the midst of a process of 'turning inside out'. Of remembering the truth of what we have forgotten. And of releasing the rest.

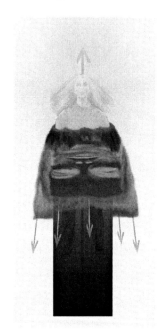

Energetically, we must 'come home into our bodies'. For it is through our bodies that our consciousness awakens.

Death is the relinquishing of the energy of the body. It is a decaying. A separation - of body from *consciousness.* Ascension is the receiving of the body. The enfolding of its energy into our consciousness. Ascension is the implosion ... of our truth into our *Light.*

'turning inside out'

♥

In these early days of seclusion I was stunned by the magnificence of what was being revealed to me. I realized that … most people would not believe what I was remembering. Because it was *so positive.* I began to realize that, at least in western culture, the only teaching or prophetic symbol for 'great change' is that of armageddon. We have no collective 'vision' of a positive transformation of great magnitude.

This is what I was receiving. The symbolic memory of the Dove, and its richly layered levels of *meaning.*

How did we lose this? Was it colluded out of our memory?

♥

We are living in an unprecedented Time in human history.[6] A Time wherein the Veil – the energetic cloud which holds our minds in the grip of 'sleep' – is becoming transparent, visible, seen and known. Recognized, for what it is. And thus 'as above' begins to meet – to truly meet - 'so below'.

This is a time of ultimate co-creation between the 'seen' and the 'unseen' worlds.

---

[6] Jesus' lifetime was a 'prior attempt' at this, though it was aborted - as it evidently was 'too soon'. More on this later.

'white rope ladder'

What this means in practical terms is that: neither will other beings or intelligences 'rescue' us from the destructive forces which we have evoked and allowed on planet Earth. Nor do we exist in a vacuum, devoid of guidance and celestial support.

We are being called to become *partners in evolution* - with unmanifest consciousness.

We - and disincarnate intelligence together - are the power.

As above, so below.

The seen.   And the unseen.   Unite.

♥

I was given a clear image of the 'mechanics' of interpersonal awakening. I was shown 'the ladder'.

A vertical, white rope ladder.

In ascension - the awakening of humanity - the physics, the principles 'work' like this: Those consciousnesses more awake than I, they reach a hand down, to guide me up. I reach a hand down, to guide others less conscious than I up, higher, towards me. Hand over hand, we assist each other. We lead each other ... *'up'*.

♥

All consciousness is involved in the awakening that we are now amidst. Nothing is left out. *All is included.*

♥

The wake. The wake is directly related to critical mass (which was shown to me even more clearly, later).

As each of us heals, and thus awakens, we create an energetic wake 'behind' us. Just like a canoe, or a beaver, or a loon swimming on a lake. Or a cross country skier breaking trail. The work of the one to break the trail is arduous. The second skier ... glides much more smoothly, with much less effort. By the time the third and fourth skiers glide along, they have no comprehension of the work it took to break the trail.

Consciousness is like this. Not everyone needs to do the same degree of work to heal.

We are all inextricably connected. Like parts of a mobile, we are all linked. The healing of one effects the overall healing of the whole. The work 'I' do, you benefit from. And vice versa.

'the wake'

And so, there is a sequencing to the collective awakening. Some of us, for various reasons, are *seeming* to awaken sooner, more fully.[7]

Those who do the preliminary healing work slick the trail for others to follow. Not everyone needs to be aware of everything to the same degree. We all benefit from each other's healing and awakening advancements.

♥

We are all a part of a great jigsaw puzzle. We each play a role - a vital role - in this. We each are a piece of it. **No one and no thing is left out.** There are no 'outsiders' in the great awakening. Nothing goes 'Home' without the whole.

♥

The jigsaw puzzle is the 'Dove'. The great vehicle.[8]

---

[7] Like the great powers of nature, all humans are consistently awakening 'just beneath the surface of their eyelids', like a collective water level rising. It is occurring, though it is imperceptible to the untrained *eye*.

[8] More on this later.

♥

"The Light is underneath, now. The Light is underneath."

To understand this ... is to *recognize where we are on the collective Map.*

It means that ... *shadow can no longer exist.*

I was told this, a vital proclamation, at a very precise juncture in seclusion. Did the two moments coincide, in 'Time'? Or was I simply ready to know this now, becoming aware of something recently happened - or about to happen - then?

Remember that some, perhaps much of what I was being remembered - in seclusion and since - was / is 'light years ahead'. On the energy levels, it has already taken place. It is 'in the bag', so to speak. It will merely take 'Time' for it to become evidenced, here on Earth.

"The Light is underneath."

It means that *nothing can 'hide' anymore.* Gradually, in its perfect orchestration of 'Time', all that was hidden is being revealed. All consciousness - and thus all form (which is a manifestation of consciousness) - is becoming transparent.

Transparent.

♥

In a simple understanding of this 'Vision' I was being shown - this Vision of the current evolution of humanity and the Earth - we are becoming 'naked souls'. The Earth is becoming, through the 'turning inside out' of consciousness. And through its twin - the 'Light being underneath'. The Earth is becoming 'safe'. For us to 'walk as naked souls', again.

Unprotected. For there is no danger.

In fact, duality is dissolving. It is 'meeting in the middle'. Opposites are dismantling. The centre is the pure state of consciousness. This is where we are returning 'to'.

♥

There has been a Veil. (This will be more clearly explained in future pages ...)

Like gasoline on the surface of a lake, it has effected confusion in human consciousness. Liken it to this: This 'gasoline' has deflected, and fractured, and distorted Light – which is the pure communication of 'God' and of all higher consciousness with us.

Imagine a pebble at the bottom of a pond. And a flashlight shining, directly to touch the pebble. The presence of the Veil - the 'gasoline' - has effectively blocked the Light from reaching the pebble. It has been deflected off, in other directions. It has been split, into a diminished message. It has been distorted, completely confused.

This Veil is being removed now. It is being overcome.

The question now is: Will humanity recognize the Light when it reaches them? Will their battered and confused brains and nervous systems be able to tolerate the purity of this Light? Will they *remember* it, in their arcane, deep, primal *soul* Knowing?

♥

To receive the purity of 'God' - of our awake, higher consciousness - we must fortify our physical and psychological systems. Simply put, we must 'cleanse'.

For any impurities in the system will react to the pure Light's potency. We will become 'ill'.

I learned this, through experience. Numerous times during seclusion, my guides informed me that they were 'amping me up'. That they were quantumly increasing the amplitude of Light which was flowing through me.

I believed them, as I had discerned their integrity over and over again.

They also explained, in each of the first number of instances of this, that they were simultaneously grounding me to *counterbalance this increased Light.* To anchor it, to ballast it 'through' me. Just like an electronic system has a 'grounding' wire to ensure that it doesn't 'short', my guides increased the strength of my grounding 'wire'.

As I became more 'intermediate' in the processes taking place in seclusion, more of a ... 'partner' than a student, I was strong enough for them to 'show' me what they were doing.

On a couple of occasions, they told me that they were about to increase the amplitude of Light I was running, yet *they wouldn't increase my grounding quite enough to match this.*

I felt ill. I felt like I can only imagine radiation sickness might feel like. On one of these occasions, I felt like 'I' was about to dissolve. My particles were vibrating so fast that 'I' would no longer exist as a distinct entity. At that moment of recognition of *what was happening,* they immediately increased my grounding to balance the increased voltage of *Light.*

♥

On more and more frequent occasions, my guides would ask me to 'imprint' what I was experiencing. As I was, at all times now, in a state of varying degrees of trance, I was somewhat 'dependent' on them to give context and a sense of safety to my experiences. Without them - in the 'normal' world, and in the midst of the glue of other people's beliefs - it would not be easy to retain my connection, my 'wiring', to the level of truth which I was currently perceiving.

So they would hold me, lovingly motionless, for what seemed like hours at a time. To 'imprint'.

To imprint was to consciously sear into my physical awareness the state of consciousness that I was in. To remember, *in me,* this physical Ariole, what they were so adeptly demonstrating to me 'energetically'. To wire into my physical awareness the enormity *and reality* of the energetic realms.

Inprinting would neutralize the human doubt.

Later they would begin to 'test' me, to fortify me. And if they had not taught me this - how to imprint the potency of my awakening experience - I can only wonder if I would have been stranded between two psychic shores.

♥

One day they asked me to lie down on the sofa, and to perceive into my sanity.

They explained to me that, if I remained conscious of my sanity, I would never lose it.

They took me to the brink, to recognize how and why so many great 'thinkers' had gone insane. They had not been grounded sufficiently for the consciousness that they were running. The electricity running through them became too strong. They 'shorted out'. They went crazy, by psychiatric terms.

I recognized in awe yet again the brilliant orchestration - the preparation of my life. I had been led to fall in love with a physical art form which *held* me in my body. Dance, and a daily Yoga practice since the age of fourteen, brought me into my body every day. These two physical, spiritual practices actively, effectively strengthened my grounding wire. Without this, I don't know that I could have withstood the potency of my waking up.

It was one of those moments of 'cosmic laughter' amidst the ultimate seriousness of my 'mission'. (Wait a moment - the cosmic laughter will come!) My mission - of awakening as much as I could, as swiftly as possible, in as short a period of time as I could tolerate, before I would have to 'return to civilization'.

The 'cosmic joke' was that, in this lifetime, I had chosen (and they had chosen me) a psychiatrist father and a social worker mother. As I stretched into even greater awakening, I would have people close to me who had known me all my life. Protected from the limited scope of much psychiatric thinking and pathological labeling, my parents would be able to recognize my *increasing sanity*.

For I knew that I was in fact becoming *more sane*. **As long as I stayed grounded**. As long as I stayed grounded … in my guides waking me up … I was becoming even more sane.

'overlapping wakes'

As I understood this 'container' of my mission, I became more and more committed. I understood the principle of the 'wake'.

The more that I could awaken, the less 'work' others would have to do. Just like a lead cross-country skier breaking trail. It was a simple principle of inverse mathematics. Because we are all so inextricably linked *energetically* - all of us - the more I could awaken, the more they would naturally be affected by my healing, and that of others, too.

And I understood, too, that awakening, and critical mass, are logarithmic. They aren't 'adding or multiplying', as in simple mathematics. ... In other words, the potency of awakening is like a homeopathic remedy. A minute quantity has a potent effect.

♥

As I continuously relaxed in the presence of my guides, I could sense their relief in having successfully guided me this far. I then realized even more astutely the intricacies of waking someone up. All of the temptations they needed to guide me around. The lulling forces that could so easily have kept me from *hearing them.*

♥

It was around this time that I was given a simple understanding of how guidance - on the grand scale - works. It's like a huge conference organizing centre. 'Missions', or, in more preparatory terms, 'intuitions and insights' are 'dispatched'. Given to individuals.

If they receive the message, and heed it, and move it into action, then they are fortified by this experience. They swiftly learn to trust their intuition - their guidance - and they begin to be given intuition and guidance of greater and greater magnitude and implications.

If they don't receive the message - if the Veil, and/or their resistance, is too thick - they are given a grace period in which to receive it. If this fails, and/or if they receive the message and yet choose to ignore it - to *not act on it* - then the 'mission' is given to someone else.

As a result, the whole mobile[9] is constantly, delicately re-balancing and shifting, moving humanity - the *Dove* - into the awakened state. Re-balancing is never a re-turn to a past state of balance. It is constantly evolving, the 'mobile' spiraling to higher and higher levels of collective frequency.

The complete orchestration of the awakening waits only so long for each of us as individuals to be 'leaders'. We are all given our 'grace periods'. If we choose to stay in slumber, for that moment we are allowed to. Eventually, the critical mass will wake us up - *all* of us.

♥

What distinguishes this Time, now, in 'history', is this. We are at the Time of the mass awakening.

---

[9] In systems, each aspect within the system affects it in its entirety. Just as in a mobile, even the slightest movement effects a wavelike dance of the whole as it finds its new homeostasis - its 'new balance'.

There have been numerous (though relatively speaking, only a handful) of people who have become enlightened - or 'awake' - since the dawn of 'Time'.

What distinguishes 'now' from all past Time is that now, we are in the swell, the pull, the 'turning inside out, of the whole'.

We are on the brink of the awakening of all human consciousness from the 'dream'. This is the mass awakening. And the implications of it are almost unbelievably positive.

♥

Only Light passes through the cosmic birth canal on the journey back 'Home'. Not even a shard, a sliver of forgetfulness, or malevolence, or manipulation can pass through.

Turning inside out. Everything exposed. That which was hidden - seen. Absolutely clear. Transparent. No more 'secrets'. No more manipulation. All energy revealed.

Shadow - being lit into full wakefulness. Consciousness - becoming fully en-*light*-ened.

What does it mean to be enlightened?

From our vantage here, it is to release all negative attachment. To regain our original state of ultimate benevolence. A reference point in understanding this is 'becoming an Ascended Master' - one who is fully awake, and thus fully in service to awakening all of the others - to the awakening of the Whole. This - enlightenment - is the ultimate in 'generosity'.

♥

I was taught how to recognize essence, through dreams. Every other night, I would have an 'essence dream'. In it, there would be a central character and, once I was aware of 'the dream', I would recognize that my task was to identify this character.

With each of these dreams, the character's 'disguise' became more elaborate. At times it was hilarious! None of the physical characteristics, or the dress, would reveal the character to me. I had to sense deeper, to perceive deeper, to recognize who it was.

Each time, in these dreams, it was Alessandro. He seemed to take such delight in 'playing'. In being the source of this joyous form of my learning.

When I awoke from each dream, I would 'sit' with it - with the flavor of the energy, until I could penetrate it with my awareness. This was how I was taught to recognize essence - the distinguishable, unaltering energy beneath the 'mask'.

♥

There was humor amidst the intrigue and seriousness of these 'teachings'.

When I began to realize 'where I was', in the presence of my guides, I recognized that I was, for the most part, completely willing and courageous. Yet ... when I sensed that 'brooms might fly', I sensed a limitation in me.

"Please, no brooms!", I joked, sensing that my guides could easily send them flying through space. They knew that I was serious. I could handle almost anything, in terms of the awakening of my perception. *As long as there were still clearly two realms: my physical self, and my energetic awareness - my awakening consciousness.* If brooms had begun to fly, even in jest, with no other humans to speak with to 'download' my experience, I was afraid that the fine line of my sanity could be bridged.

So I set perhaps the only boundary to my guides that I ever felt I needed: "Keep my energy awarenesses in the realm of energy, for now."

Don't cross this over into 'tricks' in the physical.
No flying brooms!

♥

Downloading. This is a practical application of the 'white rope ladder'.

I receive awakening - retrieved, regained comprehension of what I had forgotten. I receive it *not to keep it*. **I receive it, to give it away.**

To keep my system clear, so that I can receive higher and higher amplitudes of consciousness, of Light, I must give away what I am given.

As I remember, I must share. In 'giving it away', I do two things. I make space to receive more. And I become more buoyant. I 'rise up'.

As I pass the awakened consciousness, the comprehension which I've received down - just like in a family tree - I then float up to higher rungs.

Energetically (this is physics - metaphysics), as I 'give away' consciousness, I vibrate at a higher frequency of Light. It's much like distillation. In practical terms, this means that I rise up.

What happens if I 'hold on'? My system becomes clogged. It becomes sluggish. I actually drop down. Potencies of light become deflected by this 'film' in me. I may become ill.

It's very practical, this teaching.

Waking our consciousness up is a very embodied, practical thing.

♥

It was getting close to the day when Beth would return. And seclusion was evidently not nearly over. In a sense, it had just begun.

So I would have to move location.

To undertake this would require enormous trust, for - up to this point in seclusion - I had heard my guides in the privacy and quiet of this log cottage. How would I be able to maintain this fragile connection to them, 'out in the world'?

"We're going for a walk, lille one." It was Shakey.

"What?!?" I was sure I must have heard him inaccurately.

"Lille one, we're going for a walk."

I felt fear in the pit of my stomach. I had become absolutely comfortable with this 'realm' that I was in, here in the safe confinement of this cottage. How would I manage when I encountered people *who could not see my guides?*[10] Would I be strong enough to maintain connection with them, even when people tried to engage me in 'their' conversations? Could I maintain a link to *both worlds at the same time?*

That's why Shakey and my guides were taking me on a walk.

It felt like baby steps, at first. Not in terms of my feet - in terms of my mind.

---

[10] See "Field of Dreams", the scene where the brother-in-law cannot see the players, for an understanding of this.

I was living in an 'inner' world. A very, very real world of consciousness awakening. And yet, to the average eye, I looked completely 'normal'. Meaning, I *looked like I was in the world that they were in.*

This is when I really realized that you can't fit a ball onto the head of a pin. No matter how diligently I might try to explain, no one who was not yet open to comprehending would or could grasp what I was experiencing. *They would have to be open, and sufficiently wired.* Without this, they would not grasp it.

We walked. With each step, with each 'jostling' of my body, I intentionally connected the wires - 'up'. Up. I intentionally linked myself, with the strata of communication, of my guides.

It was hard work, essential work. This, in its essence, would become my work for the next fifteen years.

♥

The real purpose of seclusion was to increase my trust. To reawaken and increase my trust in the truth - in the unseen.

To accomplish this, my trust would have to be cracked open, first.

Why trust? Why was trust - mine or anyone else's - so important?

The horizontal to the vertical. 'We have to heal the horizontal, to heal the vertical'. We have to heal our 'pasts, and our long pasts' (meaning woundings and weakenings of trust in this lifetime, and former times) ... 'in order to heal the vertical - our trust in God'.

I got it. So simple. Like a verité - a glistening diamond of wisdom - sitting right before my eyes.

How can we awaken to realize that God has not betrayed us? How can we release our global, cultural perception, our rigid belief in 'God' as being wrathful, the source of our misery?

The only way for us to heal our relationship with God is to heal our relationship with Life, first. Try it, get into it. You'll discover what I mean.

♥

I sensed it. It was a pervading, gently gnawing sense, all the time.

"Why is God so sad?" I asked Shakey, several times. Eventually, he answered me. "You will know, lille one. In Time."

I would have to wait. All I could do for now was to sense this tremendous sadness, to be aware of it. This sadness ... in God.

♥

My guides taught me a lot - they led me into vast and intricate understandings - by studying the poetry of Alessandro. It blew me away. I had never been one to listen to the lyrics in 'poetry set to song'. It had always been the music itself which moved me.

So when Shakey led me to the albums of Alessandro's music that 'I apparently had'. And that 'I'd apparently brought', amidst the thirteen items of luggage that I'd transported to Blind Bay. I discovered that this 'man', his *soul who was my guide,* he was most definitely awake.

I realized an important phenomenon through this studying. That … many artists 'channel' their work. That … *they're not consciously aware of what they are saying.*

I could recognize this in my own choreography. One of the solos which 'I'd' created was a perfect example of this. I choreographed it, rehearsed it, premiered it, and videotaped it without any conscious understanding of what it was about. It was only when people viewed the videotape in my presence and asked poignant questions that I could *see it.* That I could see what this dance was saying.

And so I could grasp, when Shakey explained to me that 'Alessandro' - the man himself - was not yet conscious of the full meaning of what he was singing. His 'lyrics' - the expression of his higher self, his soul - they were awake.

And yet I sensed, both to my relief and my dismay, that he himself - perhaps the closest ally I had in my awakening - he was not yet as awake as I. Just beneath his eyelids - I could *sense it*. His soul ... ready to burst through. Like a racehorse at the gate, being kept in check, 'til it was his *Time*.

. In fact, we were 'leap frogging over each other'.[11] He had become more awake than I, in order to scribe these lyrics. He had written them, partly, to give me courage to remember what my guides were so diligently and patiently revealing to me.

Now, I was awakening more than he. And I had to trust that, just as in all applications of the 'wake' and of critical mass, that my awakening would further awaken him too.

Why was this so important? Because I was being shown - *I was remembering, in the very cells of my own being* - that he and I 'sat'. At the entryway of An. That in another aspect of our beings, we were the Gatekeepers, of An.[12]

I could feel the precariousness of my awakening - the vital nature of sequencing, of timing. I would be shown this, 'exterior' to me, numerous times in the future. That to awaken someone ahead

---

[11] I was shown the 'sitting beside God, just before incarnating into this lifetime' memory again. This Time, I noticed that ... a few 'moments' before I left God's side to descend down to Earth ... Alessandro did. He and I were 'paired' with God. And ... the awakening plan called for him to incarnate first, some ten Earth years ahead of me.
[12] More on the significance of this later.

of their Time, is to abandon them in a realm which cannot understand them.

I trusted and prayed that Alessandro wouldn't leave me, awake and stranded. Like so many of his lyrics, 'ironically', had spake for him.

♥

I was shown a very clear vision - of Alessandro and I.

We were on a large stage, before thousands of people.

He was, as we faced the audience, on the left. He sat, eyes closed, deep in trance. He was ... downloading energy, consciousness, and ... passing it, horizontally, to me. His function was vital beyond visibility. If I had tried to receive, and to communicate without his presence, not as much potency of Light - of truth, of memory - could be expressed.

I stood, downstage and to his right. What he channeled to me came out through my voice.

I realized that ... my voice, on these occasions, was sounding a language which I had not 'learned'. It was ... *'an ancient language - which we've all forgotten, yet which we all know.'*

The energetic placement of people relative to each other, my guides explained, was of utmost importance. In the language of visions such as these, always, the being on the left is the 'channel', the one who downloads from the higher dimensions, stepping the frequency of communication down to the point where it can be received here, on this level, on 'Earth'.

The person on the right is the 'active one', the one who is the bridge to the human world of consciousness. The 'voice'.

♥

One of the most beautiful 'teachings' - or rememberings - that my guides facilitated for me was of tantric communication between light bodies.

I was already aware, more and more so, of myself as being simultaneously a 'light body' - a translucent body of light - as I am a physical body. I understood, more and more, that our physical bodies are vibrating at higher and higher frequencies so that ultimately, they will 'merge' into our light bodies again.

And so I had become, in this brief few weeks, very comfortable with my experience of myself as my light body.

So when they transported me into memory of 'tantric dancing', it was a thrill.

As light bodies, we are expressions of love. Fully and completely. Having transcended duality, we no longer feel or express any state other than bliss, joy, love.

Having transcended the reductionist functions of digestion, excretion, and procreation, our entire being is a sensory organ. Sensation, and feeling (physical and emotional) is no longer limited to or focused in particular regions. *Our whole being is an organ of love. A communicator of love.*

In the existence or state of being of light beings, there is no gravitational pull. It's like being in a lunar landscape, yet with no physical 'planets'. It is pure Light. Pure infinite space.

My guides led me into experiential remembrance of 'porpoise diving', a most joyous dance of two (or more - like a 'pod') light bodies gliding over the surface of each other's beings.

And somersaulting, and flipping joyously together through infinite Light space. It was ultimate play.

They also led me to re-experience 'swimming'. Where one light body surrenders into another light body, filling them up with their Light. And where another light body surrenders into you, filling you up internally - like a balloon fitting inside another balloon - with their Light.

A most amazing experience.

♥

There was also a very difficult experience which my guides led me through. They orchestrated it a couple of times.

I could tell how difficult it was for them to lead me through this - as if there was no way around it, no option that could accomplish the same result.

As I've mentioned, the entire purpose of seclusion, seen from one angle, was to increase my trust. To assist me to heal my own horizontal path, and to awaken me to the existence of the vertical. To awaken me to the truth of God, a realm of consciousness much more than the 'one God' as we have understood 'him'.

To achieve this would require tremendous courage, because I would be walking out of conventional ways of thinking in order to perceive and to remember all of this - in its mind-boggling, awesome, belief shattering nature.

Even more important from the vantage of the 'big picture' was that I increase my trust - in the potency and the reality of the 'Map' I was gradually being revealed. A 'Map' so spell-binding that most humans would discard it as being 'impossible' - *simply because it is so positive.*

In the face of this disbelief I would need to maintain my trust in my fellow humans' ability to, on various levels, sense this 'Map' too. And it would be imperative that I maintain my trust in 'God' and all the higher consciousnesses. For they were my life cord - the ones who *knew* this Map and were revealing it to me, that I would reveal it to others.

And as the Veil had so effectively convoluted our trust and faith in God, this would be an enormous undertaking - not only for me - it would be a colossal undertaking of trust for humankind.

To be a consciousness 'leader' in service to this vision - to awaken to it and to scribe it as I was being shown it - I would have to completely, without any error of doubt, trust in God. 'God', and the realm of even higher consciousnesses beyond …

My guides explained that sometimes, to heal a deeply embedded wound, one must open it up.

They devised an ingenious way to do this. They called it 'mock betrayals'.

They would set me up, to fall. They would lead me to believe something with all my heart. And then it wouldn't happen. They would encourage me to vest my entire trust in what they were preparing me for, and then it wouldn't transpire.

I felt *so abandoned* … each time this happened. I felt so remarkably alone.

This was precisely what they were setting up.

For the human psyche has come to believe, over Time - through the repeated pain and struggle of Time - that we have been abandoned by God.

My guides had to take me out on a limb, and then induce a cutting sense of abandonment, in order to open up this wound.[13]

Each time (this happened three times), I would be very, very tender afterwards. I would want to withdraw from them - yet - where could I go? I had no one in the flesh who could comprehend where I 'was'. My only option was to continue forward. And to do this meant that I continue to let my guides lead me.

They would keep their gentle distance, observing my anguish. And I could feel theirs. They did not like doing this, evoking my deep psychic pain.

Gradually they would ask ... if they 'could explain to me what had happened'. And gradually, because I could sense their sincerity and the all-pervasiveness of their benevolence, gradually I would allow them to come near.

And each time, it absolutely blew me away anew. Each time, it became crystal clear that *what they had done. Was to shatter the world view which they had just successfully built for me. The world view which they had painstakingly, over the course of days and weeks, built and drawn me to see and trust.* And now they had

---

[13] On some level, either conscious or unconscious, wounds need to be 'opened up' – awakened – in order for the energy contained and fossilized in them to be released. It is through this process that all of our energy ultimately comes to be – to rest - in the present. This is what peace is – both inner peace and outer peace. Peace arises when "all energy is in the present ... and in being in the present it is free to move forward".

shattered it. Like priceless china, painstakingly hand crafted by rare masters, they had smashed it on the floor.

At this point in their 'explanation' I would always feel relieved and lost. Relieved because I was suspended, for a moment, without any world view. No thought. No concepts. No impressions. No activity in my brain. Peace.

And lost because, without a world view, there was no interface with 'what is'. Here in form. No bridge. And I was still in form. I needed a paradigm in which to exist.

There would be silence for a few moments.

And then, ever so gently, and patiently, and swiftly (for we had done this once, twice, three times before, and the framework was laid) … they would begin to construct for me the new world view.

What I had sensed was lost, was not.

All that previously was, was incorporated - in its essence - into this new, more composite and inclusive 'mobile'. This new, more relevant, more coherent 'Map' of what is.

Every single time - it blew me away.

This, more than anything, fortified my trust in my guides. The process via which they led me. The amazing, mind blowing genius of how they coordinated my awakening. How they set things up in the physical, as preparation.

They had long ago superseded 'my' ability to create. They had long ago surpassed my ability to imagine, let alone coordinate.

And this, too, increased my awareness of my sanity. For 'I' was not creating this experience. I was not creating them. They existed 'outside of me'. And I was not creating what they were revealing to me. They gave me just enough 'anchors' in the physical in terms of evidence, for me to carry on.

Remember, trust and courage. Trust and courage. As much as to awaken my paranormal 'comprehension', I was in seclusion to increase my (our collective) trust and courage.

♥

They were so masterful - and varied - in how they spoke to me.

Firstly, with time, I was able to discern 'who' was speaking. They were on different stratas of consciousness. And so they could 'channel through each other'. They did this often, simply to make it easier for my nervous system. For ... consciousness 'farther out' is harder for us to hear. We aren't 'wired' for it, as easily as we are wired to perceive angels, for instance.

So on occasion God would speak through Shakey, and Shakey through Alessandro. And this would be easier for me to receive. And sometimes they spoke as a 'composite', as it wasn't really important for me to identify who the message was from. The message was the important thing.

They spoke to me in visions. And words. And movements of energy.

Often, for hours at a time, I would be held motionless, lying down. Aware that I was in trance - and comfortable with the knowing that my 'unconscious' mind was engaged - minimal if any conscious awareness would rise to the surface. In these times, my little mind was quiet.

Typically then, after what might have been hours of 'still mind', a basic understanding of what had been taking place would float into my awareness. Somewhat like a surgeon, after an operation, giving a brief layman's description of what had transpired.

I was comfortable with all this. In fact, I felt enriched by it. It felt like I was being fed - energy - on a very deep level of my being.

Later - much later - I would recognize that this phase of seclusion had prepared 'the field' of reception even more deeply in me. Such that I could later receive composite memory - chunks of memory of the 'unseen worlds' - with such clarity that I could easily articulate it. In a sense, these first few months of seclusion were the more 'gross, unconscious' levels of my consciousness awakening.

My guides spoke to me through my breath. And through involuntary movements of my head.

Basically, there were two kinds of communication between us. The information which they were conveying to me. And the questions which I was asking to them.

Sometimes, with the latter, it would be evident that the best way to facilitate this conversation was for me to ask binary response questions. Elaborate descriptions would require visions and the like. Simple 'yes and no answers' could be given through my breath and movements of my head.

It was most intriguing. A 'yes response' would be a swelling of my lungs with breath intake until I felt I was about to 'pop'. A 'no' would be a complete, prolonged vacuum. A state of no breath.

If I ever 'smarted them' - if, on rare occasion, I was simultaneously aware of the process and of the question - they would immediately shift it. On the rare occasion that I tried to 'create' their method of communication with me, I couldn't. My lungs would be held motionless. I couldn't over expand them even when I tried.

The movements of my head evolved as a means for their answering me when I was physically in motion. They were grosser - larger - and so easier to read when I was later in public. Yet they were still extremely subtle, insignificant to an onlooker's eye. *I could feel them.* And again, I couldn't willfully replicate them.

As I later discovered in the practices of dowsing and kinesiology, 'super intelligence' speaks through the body, through the Earth. When we learn to read its language, *we can speak with it.*

♥

One of the most marvelous and rare means by which my guides spoke with me - it happened only once during seclusion - was 'ping pong'.

Usually, when I was lucid in communication with them, they would need to speak with me in images, sensations, sounds, words that I could recognize. As I became more adept, I no longer needed them to 'reduce' their expression into the containers of human mind recognition.

They could then speak with me in concepts, without reducing these into images and words. Whole concepts.

And once, they didn't even reduce this far. We spoke in 'ping pong'.[14]

It was as if we were sitting facing each other. And they would … 'serve' … energy … towards my third eye.[15] My third eye would receive it … and, without 'me' decoding its contents into brain

---

[14] I later experienced something very similar in speaking with the Dalai Lama and with Lancelot •.
[15] The brow chakra, in the centre of the forehead.

comprehension ... 'I', my third eye would ... 'lob my response back'. Back and forth, a dialogue, a conversation of pure consciousness.

It *felt* amazing, like an inner massage in my third eye, waking it up.

♥

One way to understand what was taking place 'in' me during this phase of seclusion was that it was a preparation for the reactivation of lost abilities.

I had sensed months before, with my memory of 'flying', that we humans are on the threshold of collectively reactivating dormant abilities which lie latent in us.

Recent human telecommunication and transportation developments are accessible to us now as manifest technologies - tangible, logically perceivable and acceptable to our minds. *Because we used to embody these abilities.* We used to 'be' these capabilities. Without the 'gadgets'.

Teleportation, telepathy, telekinesis, creating with pure thought. Current technological 'innovations' are a bridge - to our readiness to believe. To remember, to know again, to *reactivate.* To awaken (to) our dormant psychic abilities.

Telepathy is premonisced by cellular telephones. 'Knowing without thinking' is foreshadowed by computers' 'minds'. Soon we will be able to locomote again without 'vehicles', and communicate without 'devices'. We will *be* the method of our communication and of our transportation, again.

Think of the Wright Brothers. Their genius was initially met with outright skepticism. Now, the majority of the western world has experienced jet flight.

There is a typical arc of 'disbelief' with all new 'inventions' - ideas which become technologies.[16] First, there is doubt and cynicism, sometimes rampant hostility. Then, there are the subscribers, the handful of people who can grasp that it 'could be real'. Gradually, as these leaders 'pave the way' in our collective mind, there is acceptance.[17]

♥

Within a few days it would be time to leave Beth's - the log cabin I had seen in the vision when I was ten.

I was a bit overwhelmed at the prospect of traveling - this time without a 'known destination', and *with* invisible friends - and thirteen pieces of luggage. My guides assured me that, upon departure this time, there would be much less.

---

[16] I perceive 'inventions' to be the reception into conscious awareness of that 'which already is'. At the point of 'invention' we as a species are simply ready - finally - to perceive it. It has 'arrived' in our reality.

They gave me a vision of the luggage that would stand in the doorway when I departed the cabin.

"How could you possibly ... ?!", I exclaimed. I couldn't' see how they could conceivably fit everything I still needed ... into *that?*

Sure enough, just as they had selected and guided what I would bring to this cottage, I surrendered 'my' will and let them sort and pack again. And sure enough ... just as they had shown me ... it fit. I could carry these bags to a taxi, in two trips.

♥

These little 'tests of my trust' were nerve wracking. Amazingly, I didn't feel stressed by the enormity of what they showed me hour by hour, day by marvelous, miraculous day.

Yet, when they 'set me up ... to trust them to follow through', I felt adrenaline course through my veins. For ... what if they couldn't do it? What if they couldn't do simple things, maintain simple promises, here in the physical? Promises that 'they' made to me?

I felt mild panic every time they set this kind of 'promise and premonition' situation up. And each time, when they successfully

---

[17] The majority of human communication takes place non-verbally. It is a *discussion between our unconscious minds.*

did in the physical what they said that they would do, I felt relief, awe, and an indescribable respect for them.

♥

I was a young adult, in a realm still familiar to the rich and fertile minds of children.

Kids often have 'imaginary friends'. 'Invisible playmates'.

Who are they?

Why do adults *pretend* … that they're not real?

Out of the Cabin

- Passing through 'The World'

I t was morning, very early. I had not looked at clocks in six weeks. My guides had, on my first day in Beth's cabin, directed me to 'turn them around'. And so, for six weeks, I had no clockwork sense of time.

The headlights cut through the dark and bounced up off the snow.

The taxi arrived.

Stepping out of the cottage for the first time since 'the walk', I carried, in two loads, my current luggage to the car. And the log cabin was behind me.

It was all about trust now. I still couldn't speak with anyone, because I was always in a light state of trance, and to 'leave' it would be like an electric shock to my system. So, unlike my very friendly nature, I avoided interpersonal contact with people. This felt very strange. Yet I recognized that, as long as I was being guided by these invisible guides and thus in trance, this was actually the easiest way to proceed.

Because ... no matter how lucidly I might explain what I was experiencing - what I was in the midst of ... I didn't expect anyone to really understand.

Aboard the Greyhound bus again, heading west. I had no idea where I was going, or what was 'next' in terms of what I was being led to become conscious of in this seclusion journey. When I asked my guides, they said that I could be going virtually anywhere. With a giddy sense of humor, they said that I could travel next by ferry, plane, camel, horse, moped, taxi, or many other sorts of transport. I saw their humor, yet this situation didn't feel all that funny to me. Trusting them was even more absurd than trusting my parents as a very young child. At least my parents were visible, tangible. My guides, to the normal human eye, could not be seen.

What's more, aboard the Greyhound bus they began to crack jokes with me. They were clearly so relieved to have successfully led me this far - in the 'inner' worlds of awakening, as well as in the physical world of letting go. So they were delighted, and somewhat 'loose'. I couldn't deny them this. It was quite understandable.

Yet ... the personal discipline and resistance it took for me to not burst out laughing! I was quite self aware - respectful of the people around me who couldn't 'see'.[1] I was concerned that - as they were still unaware of the piercing *reality* of what I was awakening to (they couldn't perceive it) - they would think that I was somehow 'strange'. More like crazy. I knew I wasn't. Still, I didn't want to push an argument about 'the invisible' that I couldn't yet win!

We arrived in Hope. The bus stopped. The driver said: "Everybody off!"

I felt panic inside. I was like a newborn child, insecure and uncertain how to be in the world. Every time the slightest thing changed in my environment - when I was required to physically move, while in trance - it frightened me. The trance didn't. I was totally accepting and at ease with it. It was the moving about in the world that did. I was still a neophyte in this. I still wasn't strong enough that my 'wires wouldn't get jostled loose'.[2] And ... without a direct and active connection with my guides ... where was I?

I listened in. Shakey was there, immediately with me, as he always was. He assured me that I would be fine. Nothing to worry about. "Please take everything with you", the driver said. So I lifted down my rolled up Turkish rug, which I'd placed in the rack above my head. And I walked out into the midday light.

---

[1] See again "Field of Dreams" - the scene where the in-laws cannot see the players and evidently feel they're being made fun of.

[2] Remember the film, the Veil. It is very strong, tenacious. It continually tries to deflect our connection with *truth*. It constantly attempts to thwart us. *Until we are stronger than it,* 'again'.

It was a most remarkable experience. In 'Hope', my fourth guide introduced itself.

I first noticed a new sensation, inside my physical body. It was like … a 'spatula', a giant spatula, guiding my movements, from within my own body.

In the log cottage, at Blind Bay, I had experienced something akin to this. There, I had been directed to descend into the basement. I was to place a chair, in the epicenter of the room. And I was to sit, facing the sliding glass doors so that I could align myself with 'the three trees'.

I did this. I settled in, and I closed my eyes.

Before I knew it, a 'force', evidently having entered into my body, began to lovingly, gently, 'move me'. I was not moving myself.

It was … oh so gentle, yet precise. My spine, from the tailbone up, was gently being torqued … towards the right. In precision increments, I would be spiraled, then held motionless for a moment, then spiraled again. Once the range of motion had been explored to the right, this 'inner force' gently returned my spine and my head to face forward again.

A brief moment passed, then my torso was spiraled to the left. This time the stages were much simpler, as if spiraling to the right had also aligned the left. Again the movement was complete, and the benevolent inner force returned my spine and head to face directly forward.

Everything was still. The 'force' was gone - it could not be detected. And I noticed ... that my energy centres, my chakras, were *absolutely precisely vertically aligned.* I had never, ever in my life felt so perfectly vertical. A gorgeous golden flow of energy, like honey, or maple syrup sap, flowed deliciously up my being. It was like the sound of a harp, being played inside of me.

'Cosmic chiropractics'. The words floated effortlessly into my brain. Cosmic chiropractics. I had been 'adjusted', by an invisible force.

And ever so faintly, in my mind I knew, that I could now attune even more clearly. My 'mind', it could be awakened even more precisely, and with so much greater ease.

♥

So here in Hope, as I began to be aware of the 'spatula', spiraling inside of me, it was not an entirely unfamiliar experience.

I surrendered into it, cautiously at first, discerning intently, as this feeling was 'new'. It guided me, physically, from within myself ... to walk the streets of Hope. I would approach a street corner, aware that the decision of which direction to turn was not my 'own'. I let the inner energy steer me.

It was a most fascinating 'walk', through the town of Hope. Turkish rug rolled up in my hand, this whole process was so surreptitious. I was aware that nothing about me would really look strange. I was just walking, and arcing ever so gently at the 'corners' with my turns. No one watching would ever have suspected. That I was being introduced to Antori Solaris.

'Antori Solaris'

Antori Solaris (I called it Ansy, as we became acquainted) is the 'God' of the 5th dimension.

I had already awakened clearly to understand that 'God' - the energy or intelligence that most people who relate to a singular god entity identify - is actually only the nearest in a dimensional *'trail'* of

Gods - energies like us, who remained as 'markers' along the cosmic birthing path.[3]

The God that most people relate to is the God or 'gatekeeper' of the 4th dimensional portal - or the God of the 4th dimension.[4] 'God' watches over all within 'his' dominion - all energy which exists within the Wheel of Time[5], the realm of creation of Earth, Space and Time.

I already knew, in being awakened to realize this, that what I was being 'remembered' - brought into memory of, during seclusion - would rock the beliefs of the Christian Church, not to mention many other dogmatic religions. 'God' was the most accessible, the 'nearest to us', of a beautiful string of consciousnesses just like us. The only real difference was / is that they remained as 'breadcrumbs, berries along the path'[6] to mark our way Home. And we came into incarnate forgetfulness.

So Sourcey was 'God', the gatekeeper of the 4th dimensional portal.

Ansy was the next one 'out'. The gatekeeper of the 5th dimensional portal.

---

[3] More on this later.
[4] The 'gatekeeper' of the 5th dimension is the bridge or energy 'valve' between the 4th and 5th dimensions. Dimensions are like strata - layers of higher and higher vibrational frequencies. (In truth they are omni-dimensional, existing as overlays, interweaves, though it may be easier at first for us to perceive them as distinct and separate though interconnected 'tiers'.)
[5] The Buddhist expression of samsara, the contained world of creation in which suffering exists.

Ansy was the first in my lineage of guides who didn't appear 'male' to me. Ansy was clearly neither male nor female. What we might call, simply for the purpose of language, 'androgynous'.

Ansy never incarnated. He / she / it had twelve 'dispatchees' - aspects of its energy - which journeyed closer to Earth and other universes from time to time. Yet Ansy him / her / itself never journeyed from its 'throne' - its place as gatekeeper of the 5th dimension. It was very powerfully anchored there.[7]

Ansy always spoke to me in limerick. It was rare - it only happened a couple of times - that he / she / it spoke to me directly. Usually the communication filtered through Sourcey and Shakey. Because Ansy's energy was *so pure,* it nearly burned me out. Well beyond the frequency of duality, Ansy's energy vibrates at lightning speed. On the rare occasion that he / she / it spoke directly to me, I could receive it for what felt like thirty seconds. Then, much to my chagrin, I would have to ask him / her / it to 'pull back'. I felt on the verge of nausea, unable yet to ground such intensity of pure and potent Light.

---

[6] Like "Hansel and Gretel" navigating their way through the woods.
[7] As 'ballast' for the 'volunteers' - the 'forgetful' souls confined to the incarnate and soul planes, lulled to 'sleep' by the existence of the 'Veil'.

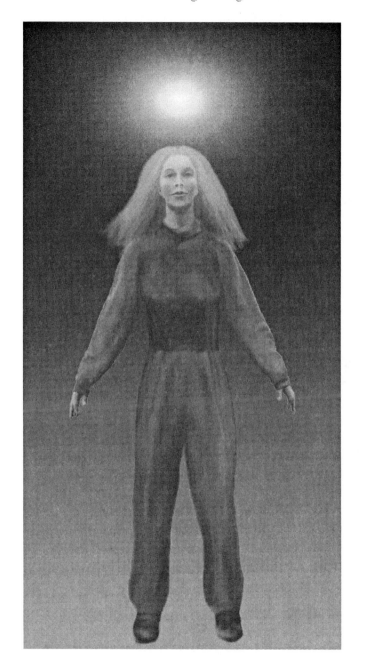

'Ariole and Ansy'

When he / she / it did speak to me directly it was always, always in rhyme. It blew me away how so much, of intricate yet essential detail, could be communicated in this way. As the communication flowed, it amazed me how it could all be conveyed in rhyme.

Rhyme is the energy of balanced didactics. Energetically, it is the pairing of the opposites, the 'filing of the pairs into the arc, two by two'.[8] It is the flowing together of the 'traffic', into One.

I knew this from another amazing experience. Towards the end of my time at Blind Bay, Shakey wrote through me. When this began to happen, I realized that he had written purely and directly through me once before. In the 'horizontal' stage of the writing of the big Book, at one point a sonnet wrote itself. It was describing an event that 'I' could remember clearly. (About costumes, and performances, and squat toilets in France!) 'I' could easily have written about this. Yet …

Words were written through me in a shape and form of mastery that I could never have written. 'I' had never written prose in this genre before. It was like a sonnet, each line with a particular number of syllables - a 'lilt'. *And in rhyme.*

---

[8] The Biblical 'ark' is the Dove in its originally intended course - its trajectory as the 'boomerang'. Both the 'arc' and the 'boomerang' are 'meta fours' - symbols of sacred geometry and the 'physics' of awakening. Shake speare, by the way, is a metaphor for the thunder and lightning - 'The Flood'. His writings were not about 'then'. They are about *Now*.

It was marvelous, meticulous, and miraculous. I still had not 'met' my guides at that point, and so I could only observe it in wonder in this section of the writing.

So on the afternoon when Shakey began, directly, to write 'through' me, I knew instantly what was taking place.

It was one of the most spell binding experiences of my entire life. It went on for two days. And then I needed help. In a way, it was a 'set up'. For me to open to Alessandro, in trust. For this is precisely when Shakey led me to 'hear' Alessandro's lyrics. To truly understand the metaphors he was speaking.

Oh, what a journey this was. I was lying in bed, propped up on my left elbow, as I was for hours during the horizontal phase of writing. In the instant Shakey began to write, I sat bolt upright.

I recognized it, because I had been led to participate in a voice workshop in which the First Folio of Shakespeare's Earthly writings had been presented. The First Folio are the original writings of Shakespeare, with his own natural, original spelling and capitalization.

Shakey wrote. And he wrote. Words, and phrases first. Then each of these, and clusters of them, were extrapolated. Meanings were layered within meanings.

The 'page', the physical journal in which I was to write these, couldn't contain it. It was, very rapidly, becoming a multi dimensional expression. As if a great code was being unlocked, a code not of 'here', but of infinite unlimited *Space*.

Words would be expanded, like an accordion, depending upon the dimension from which their expression of wisdom was emanating. The double consonants, and e endings, and underlined e endings, and capitalizations - *they all had a purpose. They were containing energy.* They were 'holding' it.

On very rare occasion, a word would be monosyllabic. When an expression was so important that its meaning was imperative to be understood, it would be a monosyllable.

And so this is how I recognized Ansy. He / she / it was the 'seat' … of the monosyllabic energy. The 'eye of the needle'. The gateway through which no fractured energy could pass. To enter Ansy's portal and rise to higher vibrations through it, all distinction must be united.[9]

I still have Shakey's journals. He was 'teaching me', in a very rapid fashion, of the energy markers which have been placed through 'Time'. The sacred sites, their 'why', *and how they effectively anchored memory. Memory of the story of 'Life'. And of the pathway Home.*

---

[9] This can be a challenging concept to grasp. Like An, the portal of Sourcey - of 'God' - Ansy's gateway cannot allow any negative energy to pass through. Negative energy (shadow) forgets itself. It must awaken to its true identity - as Light (it has temporarily forgotten this) - in order to pass through. All of these 'concepts' - these universal principles - are so simple. And yet, in their implications and their enactment, they are so *huge*.

♥

This was a remarkable, flowing journey of experience. I was beginning to long for the doorway, the opening when I could begin to share this simple magnitude resplendent with splendour and *wonder* with someone.

♥

I was in seclusion for seven and a half months. During that time, the only interpersonal interactions I had with 'humans' were purely functional - to buy transport tickets, to purchase groceries, to order a meal. And in none of those transactions was I to engage in 'conversation'. As my conversation, for now, was to be exclusively with those far more difficult to reach - my guides.

I was led, in intervals from a few days to six weeks, through Vancouver, to Parksville, to Tofino, to Victoria, to Saltspring Island, through Vancouver, to New York City. For two and a half months, I was in trance in New York City.

But before that ...

En route to Vancouver, I was given a powerful directive - like the 'Don't look back' decree on the hiking trail descent from Garibaldi Lake.

This one wasn't verbal - it didn't need to be. Every time my normally conditioned mind would have me turn my head to distractedly read the passing billboards along the highway, Ansy would hold my head motionless. I got the message. Don't be distracted. Release attachment to outside sources of information. They are not important. Turn your attention now, exclusively, to the source of true information.

Listen in, not out.

♥

Passing through Vancouver for the first time since the beginning of seclusion was mostly functional. I had to go 'through' it to get to the next quiet, remote place.

In Vancouver, the highlight experience was this. In the bath, in my tranquil hotel room across from a stadium. Ironically there were thousands of people there that night. I was so near to people, and yet so far.

I had several 'very long baths' during seclusion. Baths during which the water became cold. Baths, like the evening when I lay in my sleeping bag on the grassy knoll at Jericho Beach, coming to terms with what I was surrendering to.

This evening, in this bath, I was distant enough from the first stage of seclusion - Beth's cabin - and all that had taken place there.

I was still very much 'in' this mysterious, awakening process, and yet … That was precisely the point. I could look back now, at the past six weeks. And I could view the present circumstance, which was that I was still very much dependent on my guides to lead me in this territory of the 'inner worlds'.

Shakey appeared in my awareness. He was so tender, and kind, and compassionate as always. As if he himself could feel precisely what I was going through.

I could sense all of my other guides, gathered around me, as if this moment was a vital one. As if … I could abort this whole process, if I wanted to.

Shakey asked me, on behalf of all of them, "Lille one, do you feel like you've been kidnapped?"

I chuckled inside. His voice and his manner and the sensitivity of his question was so quaint.

"No'", I said silently, knowing that they could fully read my mind. "No." For I was willingly here. I had accepted this invitation, planned and mapped before this birth, to 'meet' them. To be the incarnate member of their consciousness awakening 'team'.

♥

Parksville was the typing of the manuscript. And the first rays of exercise in weeks. And my guides 'going out'.

The manuscript was already hundreds of pages of hand-written text, very precise in places as to spelling, capitalization, and the like. For it was a 'funnel'. The text itself, just like Shakespeare's First Folio writings, would funnel the awakening of human consciousness. He or she who entered in, would pass through a channel, a vortex of awakening by 'reading' it.

So typing it was a six week task.

My hands fell asleep. Until I realized that if I sat higher, the blood could still pump down from my heart into them. It was hours and hours of typing.

I felt relief in that very few 'new' experiences were happening. In this way it was a phase for integration. For digestion.

And a fascinating time, too, to re-read what had been written.

I was staying in a motel, right on the sea shore. So near to the sea that when the tide rolled in, the ocean nearly touched the base of my door. My room had glass windows its full width. So I could gaze out at the endless waves. Geese would swim and drift towards me. And once, I saw the 'blow' of a whale in the distance.

I managed a curtailed interaction with the Motel Manager one day. It was so different for me, very social in my nature, not to 'speak' with anyone. Not to engage in 'Earthly' conversations. Not to be 'distracted' - from the teachings and subtle energy conversations with my guides.

And so, exchanging only the bare minimum of details, I arranged with the Motel Manager to borrow a bike.

It was a most harrowing, thrilling ride. My guides were leading me, of course. And so I rode on trails that 'I' wouldn't have chosen. Bumpy, muddy. Through splashing puddles. Ugghh!!

Strange as some of these experiences were, they were so reassuring. Because ... I needed them. I needed to know, every minute of every waking day, that my guides were with me. And one of the best ways for them to demonstrate this, was to guide me in ways unfamiliar to my own.

♥

One afternoon, I had finished typing for the day. I was sitting on the floor beginning my Yoga practice. When they said, 'through' Shakey, "Lille one ... we're going 'out'."

I dreaded the sense of what this meant. "What?", I asked silently, hoping the answer would be different than what I'd first heard. "Yes, lille one. We're going out."

It was the first time, in all of seclusion, that I felt terrified. Shakey was there with me, in his compassionate and deeply understanding way. He explained that ... this would be to my benefit. That ... I needed a 'rest'. It would only be for a few hours, he assured me. *They would be back.* He explained that, in their 'leaving' me, very temporarily, *my trust in them would be strengthened.*

Yes, it was true, that they had been present in my awareness *constantly* since they'd introduced themselves to me. There hadn't been a waking moment when I didn't know, palpably and sometimes exhaustingly, that they were there. At Beth's, I had come to the stark realization that I was utterly 'naked' before them. They could see my thoughts, and read my feelings. Even my body was totally exposed to them. I was, to them, completely transparent.

So, yes, I could agree with this. It would be a 'rest'. Yet I was scared. Scared like a child whose parent steps away, out of sight. How would I cope, still 'blind', without them to lead me?

And with that, they were gone.

I felt like the poem I had written in grade eight. "And she awoke, and was alone." I missed them terribly. I *knew* they were real. It was as if … in their absence, I more strongly knew their presence.

I began to relax. I was not 'dying'. This was not terrifying. As long as I didn't have to interact with people (as I was still 'adrift from shore'), I felt calm and sure that I could handle this.

It was true. I was refreshed when they came back. It had only been two hours. Yet it felt like a long holiday. Shakey had, since the moment he introduced himself to me, spoken to me incessantly. His 'voice' was the connection. As if, on a telephone line, 'silence' would break the connection.

So he had spoken to me incessantly. I understood why, and yet it had at times been tiring. Not that I would have wished for anything else. I recognized that this 'connection' was my lifeline.

I was so grateful and relieved when they returned. I felt refreshed. And I was very ready to carry on.

♥

Tofino was a time of rest. I resisted it at first. I had grasped how valuable it was, in the scope of 'the big picture', for me to have as much courage as possible, and to awaken to as much as I could. I wanted to create as big a wake as possible. To ease the 'work' that others, not so unattached or fearless, would be called to do.[10]

I realized another aspect of my guides' brilliance. They were leading me to do something that I, culturally, had never been taught to do. To rest *before* a challenge.

I was being rested. Because there was much more still ahead.

---

[10] This is the nature of the Boddhisatva - to know the picture, to recognize the 'awakening work' required of the collective, and to do as much as they personally can, creating massive 'leverage' just as a fulcrum does. A Boddhisatva is in conscious service to the awakening of the *whole*.

♥

It was Boxing Day. And the biggest gift that they, my guides, could possibly give me was to say this: "Lille one ... It's time to write."

I had been wondering, impatiently, when the Book would be finished. The writing had stopped, completely, the moment they had introduced themselves to me. There was so much 'integration' then that needed to happen. Direct teachings that I couldn't yet write down. This had become the priority for weeks.

So now, like a nugget, a gem patiently (impatiently?!!) awaited for, I was being given the 'green light, go'. To write.

They told me that I would need only one ream of paper - that this would be 'more than enough' - to complete the Book. And one typewriter ribbon.

I was dumbfounded. They'd said, on several occasions, that this was 'the Book, of our Time'. That within the energy touched and encountered through its pages, humanity would access answers to every question ever asked.

That was an enormous proposition. I trusted that they knew 'it' - answers to all of humanity's questions throughout Time. Yet ... to write them ... in ten more pages? This is what they consistently assured me. Ten more pages was all it would take.

So we journeyed again. With fewer pieces of 'luggage' each time. This time, via Victoria, to buy the ream of paper and the typewriter ribbon. And then 'we' were off again. To somewhere much more quiet. To an off-season resort cabin, on a small island, in the midst of the sea.

I was at Booth Bay for several weeks. Eager to write, to 'complete this Book', I let my guides lead me there with enthusiasm and inner delight. I felt purpose and power. I was a fine tuned 'instrument'.

The writing of the Book was finished, so succinctly and sublimely. And yes, it was only ten more pages, as they had so clearly and confidently premonisced, 'ahead of Time'.

Trust. It was all about trust, they said. Trust was the gist of the last ten pages. The heart of the 'Book'. The heart of the human odyssey. Trust in the invisible energies. Trust … in the benevolent *Light*.

♥

I had asked, a few weeks before, to know how it was that they could predict things so clearly. How it was that they could guide me, and foresee things so accurately.

Shakey explained. He said it's like being above familiar land, in an airplane. Land that you've walked, time and again.

Being on the land, it's easy to get lost. To become 'stumped'. To encounter a boulder, or dense woods, or a stream. And to not know which way to turn. 'Land vision', he said, can be dense.

Seeing the same land - viewing it - 'from above' - this is very different. He related this as a metaphor for how they see. They are not in body (or at least, none of them are completely). They are not 'of land'. They can 'fly ... above' the land, as consciousness itself, above the vibrations of form.

And in so doing, they can see *pathways of energy.* How energy can *flow.* They can see possibilities. And probabilities. They can see clearly the 'boulders', the dense woods, the streams. Both as physical objects and as metaphors. They can see all the variables, and all of their possible interactions.

And from this *vantage,* they guide.

Like a birds' eye view.

It made complete sense to me. I had flown in a small plane over the island of our family cottage once. As a child I had come to know the trails. 'Stay on the trails', my elders always encouraged. 'Don't get lost', was the underlying message.

From the vantage of the plane, it was so obvious how one would traverse the land. For all the potential obstacles were in plain view. *They could all be seen, simply and clearly, from above.*

♥

New York. The Book was written. - It was complete. The manuscript was typed. Photocopies had been made. Most of the teachings - the 'First Installment', the underlying template of the Vision - had been received. More details of clarity would layer upon this simple foundation in the next two years.

Now I was to begin my return. My own 'homeward' trajectory - like the 'boomerang' - from the unseen back into the seen.[11] Sewing the seam … This, my own 'return from the Vision Quest'.[12]

It is said that being led on a spirit journey presents a great hurdle of courage - the first hurdle of two. Coming back to the world with the new wisdom gained is an even greater one.

---

[11] And later 'through it', back into the unseen several times again.
[12] See Joseph Campbell's lucid work on "The Hero's Journey" for diagrams illustrating the phases within the complete cycle of a Vision Quest.

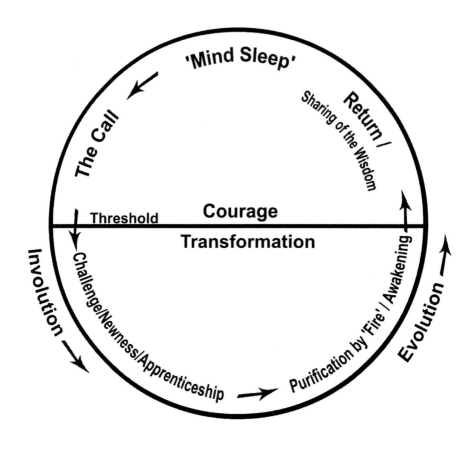

'Vision Quest' journey depiction

I was still very much in trance. In the thick of New York busyness, the thick strata of psychic, mental activity, I was still very deep in trance. There was one more, vitally significant step I was to take. I was to anchor 'the Book'.

I took a copy of it to Alessandro's New York agent. And I attempted to take a copy of it to Bantam Books.

I found Bantam on 5th Avenue. I rode the elevator up to the reception floor. And then I asked. "I'd like to speak with the person of greatest authority in your institution." They were a little stunned. I was whisked through the maze, is if they weren't certain if I was carrying a 'bomb'. Yes, this book was a 'bomb' of sorts. As it would explode much current thinking. Salman Rushdie's <u>Satanic Verses</u> had just created a global coup. So I could see why they were both voraciously curious (that's their job) and a little uneasy about what it was that I was carrying.

I carried the manuscript as a sacred object. They could see this. The way they looked at it - held within my hands - they knew it was 'gold'.

And yet …

I was taken all the way up to a Vice President. She looked as if she was going to cry. She, very apologetically, said. "We can't touch it. We can't touch it … without an agent."

I asked if I could sit down for a moment. I had to listen in. The Book had come this far. Would the apostles have needed an 'agent'? It seemed so ludicrous.

I left their tower, knowing that I was not to go to an agent. There was not to be, at least not then, a 'middle man'. Source to Source. This text - the energy within it - was to travel direct.

♥

Again, I had to be unattached. I was called to let go of any personal 'need', or want, for the manuscript to ever be published.

I had a sense that, possibly, my writing this 'Book' had allowed someone else's script to be anchored more fully. That there was a possibility that in writing it, I had 'midwifed' someone else's book.[13]

I accepted this. In service. That's what I was. I could claim no reign over the orchestration of this great awakening. As long as I listened in, as long as I discerned benevolence at the heart of all that I was guided to do, the 'big picture' would be left in the eyes of those who could see it.

No matter that I had left civilization for seven and a half months. That I had walked the ridge of sanity and had opened myself to commune with unseen guides. No matter any of this. It was out of my hands to determine whether the Book was ever to be published. In this, I would trust, too.

♥

It was in my hotel room in New York City that God visited me. And - as Shakey had promised, way back at Beth's cottage - I

---

[13] The Celestine Prophecy, a breakthrough book in western human consciousness, was released within months of this.

would finally have an answer to my question - 'Why was God so sad?'

This was the only time in all of seclusion that God - the gatekeeper of the 4th dimension - ever 'came down' from 'His' orientation up, consistently, about 45 degrees up and forward from my third eye.

This time, I was called to sit down on the bed. And ... as if He 'floated' down, just like a leaf, gently drifting to Earth from a tree ... He came and sat with me.

This was the first - and only - time that He seemed 'my size'. Always - in every other direct exposure I had with Him - He seemed infinite in His presence, infinite in His 'size'.

He came down.

And in a stillness, and a peaceful silence, we simply sat. I could *feel* His sadness. He was grieving ... a loss ... a most mournful loss.

Then, out of this *silence,* He began to speak. Just like He had, on those few occasions while at Beth's. Simple, sparse, few words. *And luminously potent.*

He explained to me, just like a best friend would, 'why' He was sad.

It was that ... He had waited, for so long, for His beloved 'children' - all of humanity ... to return Home. And ...

What if ...

What if *they did not Hear the Call?*

What if they could not, or chose not, to remember … ?

What if …

They never came Home …

?

I could feel His pain. And I could fully comprehend it.

He was not the culprit. Yet, how could humans beneath the Veil 'under stand'? How could they Know - how could they realize - that it was *the Veil,* not He, *who had abandoned them?*

He had never abandoned us. He was always there, always Loving, always patient. Just like Shakey. Patiently awaiting the precious moments when He could *receive* us - *greet* us - Home, into His state of awakened consciousness again.

I could feel as God. I could fully under stand His predicament.

And yet He had no voice. Other than through our dreams, and through our visions. *And through me.*[14]

He lingered a few minutes longer, in silence. There, as best friends - He, a radiant glow of Light - and I … we simply sat in each others' reverential company. I appreciated His trust in me. I felt Love, and respect, and Trust in Him.

---

[14] And other writers who also heard Him and 'scribed' for Him.

And then … just as in the original log cabin … He began to rise again, like a barely visible, 'tangible' vapor of Light. Up … up to where He always was. Up … above me. Up.

The Return from the Quest

It's true. I was tired. Emotionally tired. This experience had been so immense.

And … I had had no one to speak with, with 'human' ears during it.

Yes, my guides had nurtured me in a way that I had never, ever experienced in the physical world. Yet … I longed for words I could hear with 'these' ears. Sights I could see with 'these' eyes. And most importantly, touch from human hands.

My guides had hugged me, and soothed me with their voices and their love. Yet I was still in a physical body. It had become time for me to be with physical people, again.

♥

Towards the very end of seclusion, my grandfather passed away. He was the second of three grandparents who taught me about the 'transition' of so called 'death'.

My other granddad had gifted me his humor as he passed. For weeks after his 'death' he would speak to me, through humor, through nature, through flowers. He was not 'gone'. He was simply no longer physical. When he 'died', a precise moment which I knew in a spontaneous convulsion of tears, he simply left the limitation of form. He could now be in many places in many times, free to fly as spirit like his beloved gulls.

When my grandmother died later, I saw and felt a shower of light cascade up and out from her crown chakra. She was giving away her Light. In the moments surrounding her 'death', she gave away to those of us still living, her Light.

When my grandfather died, he showed me the soul plane - the vibrational frequency 'above Earth, beneath the Veil', where souls rest between incarnations.

He presented me with a vision.

He and I were walking, barefoot along a white sand beach. Immediately I knew that this beach wasn't on Earth. It was an 'etheric' beach.

As we walked, we were peaceful together in a way we had never been in this lifetime. We were equals. We were two souls who had agreed to play particular Earthly roles. It was as if ... we were now in intermission, between acts. We had taken off our 'costumes'. We knew and respected each other, as pure souls.

As we walked, I noticed something striking. He wasn't the elder man I'd known. He was youthful, agile, strong, a spring in his step.

I observed for more detail. He appeared to be ... And immediately the word 'thirty' sounded silently in my mind.

My guides then explained to me ... that when a person dies, they return to their 'resting age'.

We each have a harmonic resting age - unique to us, just like the 'sound' we make, vibrationally. Our vibrational 'sound' and our 'resting age' are identifying features unique in each one of us, as spirit. Just like our fingerprints, and our voice are, here in our physical bodies.

My grandfather's resting age was thirty.[1]

I felt inside myself. I could see and feel myself - a 'maiden'. My resting age is fourteen, with long golden hair.

♥

I gradually made my way to Vancouver, passing via my family home. My parents, and one friend in Toronto, had been my first connections 'out'. I had been guided to speak with my parents,

---

[1] Most people's resting age is in the range of twenty-eight to thirty. This, interestingly, correlates with the age when a person (incarnate) experiences their 'Saturn return' - a phase, according to Astrological teaching, of great self-awareness awakening.

via long distance telephone, from New York. This was the beginning of the transition. I had begun 'teaching'.

My parents were eager to understand, to 'learn'. I recognized in them a similar appetite to what I had felt, first hand, in seclusion. A yearning to 'know'.

This was vital to me. For in order to receive more, I had to download what I had.

I would be in trance, speaking on the telephone. They would ask questions, and answers would flow through me. Crystal clear, astute explanations of profound and difficult concepts.

It felt good to speak. It felt good to let 'teachings' flow through me, like water through a stream.

This process and the intelligence communicated through it stretched my parents enormously, as it would many people. There was no way around this. I was changed. I could not go back. What I had awakened to, would stay.

♥

When I returned to Vancouver I knew that I needed an interface - a way to have contact with people, yet privacy and the opportunity for inner silence. I had much integrating to do. My isolation needed to end, yet in a gentle way.

I worked at a new age bookstore. There, in a healing oasis, I could serve people. It would, in its energetic way, support me in the profound experiences I had just had. And it would offer me 'space'. Space to reflect. Space to weave the wonders of seclusion into this person, here now, in the flesh.

I am a bridge. I am a weaver. Sewing the seam between darkness and Light. I and my consciousness had been led ... 'out'. Now we were being led, in. Here, to Earth. Here, to share with my fellow humans the wonders I had 'seen'.

In the ensuing years, I would be led to weave out - and in, and out again - several times. Each Time, the distance would become shorter. Just as in sewing together two shores. The tighter the thread, the less distance between them. My first 'out' was seclusion, my first 'in' was my return from it. The next outs were less 'secluded', the next ins were more 'integrated with society'.

Sewing the seam, out into the invisible realms of infinite wisdom. In, like a parent bird, feeding its young.

Sewing the seam of consciousness. From darkness ... into *Light*.

♥

After about eight months of working in the bookstore, I received my next call. It was the Earth Summit.

Standing at the counter, facing the many magazines with headline stories of the upcoming United Nations conference, I 'knew I needed to go'. I had to *be there*. By miracle again, enough money had been saved in my bank account to pay the way.

I went, as an independent citizen. There are many organizations that I could have represented, as a delegate. Perhaps in the official UN conference. Or at the 'Global Forum', the parallel non-governmental conference.

I went to observe. To see from 'above'. From outside, from inside - to witness, to learn. To learn what is working. And what's not. Who is doing what. And where are the gaps.

On the flight home, I knew that I was to let go my security again. I was to convene a 'Post Earth Summit Conference', to share the wealth of Rio.[2]

I lay in bed, morning after morning, being shown the format that the conference was to take. Similar to the way in which I had been 'dictated' the details of my solo tour.

It was to begin with a large circle. No podium. No highlighted guest speakers. No microphone. Everyone would be respected as having wisdom.

---

[2] The United Nations Earth Summit Conference took place in Rio de Janeiro, Brazil. While there, I also journeyed into the Amazon, a place and an experience which I can only describe as 'wisdom hanging thick in the air'. It was a Timeless, speechless experience. Immensely profound.

I had met a First Nations elder who would bless the proceedings. A talking stick was passed. As long as it pertained to the Earth Summit - the experience and learning gained from being there, questions posed by those who had not been there, and the like - everyone had their turn to speak.

Following this, the day opened into a series of smaller circles, each evolving like a larger and larger ripple in a pond of inquiry, discovery, and visioning. At intervals, the circles would come back together as the larger whole.

At the lunch break, half the people left, uncomfortable with the unfamiliar context of the event. The other half glowed. "We've been waiting for this!" they exclaimed. They'd been waiting for an inclusive process, one in which cooperation, circles, and the non-hierarchical nature of wisdom were welcomed and understood.

This 'conference' evolved into a non-profit society whose activity was to leap frog over people's perception that they, personally, were not creative. That they, personally, couldn't 'problem solve'.

As Margaret Mead so aptly stated, everyone contributes to solutions. It is the butterfly effect, and the accumulation of all the little droplets which collectively create the change. It is the shifting, by a miniscule degree, of the compass that *alters the course.*

And so we initiated 'initiatives', events and processes and discoveries that allowed people to access their vision. To 'see' positive alternative futures. We had architects and visual artists paint and draw what people described. We had enormous canvases, and paints, and artist facilitators assisting adults and youth and children to create murals depicting positive alternative futures.

And all the while, I knew that I would be called again. I tried to the best of my ability not to let this non-profit society - its members and its Board - depend on me. To survive - to be sustainable - it needed to not need me. Inside myself, I quietly knew that my journey was not complete. There would be 'another chapter', soon. I would know when, in the instant I received 'the call'.

♥

The call - the next call - came in several stages. There was the Conclave of Michael. There were the conference calls. And there was the 'Second Installment of the Vision'.

I found myself flipping through a spiritual magazine. And there, I came across the ad.

It was like being called to Jacob's Pillow. And the Stein Festival. And the Earth Summit. I knew I had to go.

Without effort I came across other people whom I hadn't previously met who were going. I arranged to drive with them. It was in Banff - the 'Conclave of Michael'. At the majestic Banff Springs Hotel.

This was my first direct, conscious connection with the energy of the Archangels. Little did I know then, that there was so much more to come.

Banff is apparently considered to be the energetic 'seat', the etheric throne, of Archangel Michael.

There were - just like at a conference - lectures and seminars. Also a passion play. And an initiation ceremony.

For the ceremony one evening, all who wished to attend were to dress entirely in white. This was easy for me. I had worn virtually only white since I'd emerged from seclusion. There were thousands of white candles lit in an expansive, long hall.

People were ushered in in silence. Not a word was to be spoken.

I had never participated in a ritual ceremony like this before. And I truly knew no one there. So I followed my instincts, participating whenever my discernment showed me that it was appropriate for me to do so.

There were several thousand of us, sitting silently in rows, facing an altar of flowers and Light.

Sitting in my chair, unbeknownst to anyone else's awareness, I began to feel it. I now know to call this 'mudra currents'. Similar to the 'cosmic chiropractics', yet different, I knew I had no reason to be alarmed. Just intrigued.

I could feel currents of energy, 'surfing' the surface of my body. And gradually, slowly, my hands began to rise. And surf on them.

It was a most delicate, graceful ballet of the hands, riding on the waves of unseen energy, like a kite flying in the wind currents, or an eagle spiraling.

Apparently we were all asked to stand. This was a window, an opportunity for me to cast a glance around. No one else seemed to be experiencing these 'mudra currents'. Nor did anyone else seem to notice that I was.

I felt freer now, more courageous. Knowing that somehow I was, in the midst of this crowd, being granted privacy, I allowed the mudra currents to continue without self awareness.

My right hand traced three circles, counter clockwise, around my face. Then, slow motion, delicate, soft, it made the motion of the cross.

I knew … I was in the presence of Jesus. When my hand circled my face, three times, I saw his.

I didn't tell anyone of this experience. It was like - seclusion being presented - in plain view. No one seemed to notice.

♥

One evening there was a passion play in the theatre. The Conclave[3] organizers had known that I was a professional dancer. They asked me to perform the role of Lakshmi, as this was a passion play of the story of the gods.

One day in rehearsal, the cast was divided into two sections - the 'Light', and the 'Dark'. We were apparently going to enact the war.

The director arbitrarily drew a line down the centre of the rehearsal stage to make the division. I was, initially, in the cast of the dark. It felt so wrong to me. As we had been asked to bring black and white clothing for these particular costumes, and I had been guided to give away anything black, I simply said that I only had white clothing with me. This apparently sufficed. I was moved to the side of the 'Light'.

The staging was organized. We were given our cues. The 'Dark' was to physically oppress against the Light. And the Light ... was supposed to fight back.

My body froze. Not in a sense of shock, or fear. It froze in the sense of immobility. I had never received such a clear, easy to discern physical message before. It was obvious. My body would not move.

---

[3] A Conclave is a secret spiritual gathering. This one was 'advertised', yet only those who recognized its significance would Know it and feel called to go.

I discretely removed myself from the rehearsal hall and made my way to my hotel room. I lay down on the bed, and I listened in. What was going on? What was I being taught? What was I being shown?

Light need not fight. Or justify itself. Truth is.

I wrote a note to the Director, explaining that I could not perform in that scene. I disclosed why, unattached to whether or not he would 'see' it, and understand it, too.

♥

I entered one of the seminar rooms - late, as I'd just come from a rehearsal. There was a man at the front of the hall, preparing to show a series of slides. This man, Dr. Frank Stranges, had apparently worked in the White House and had met the people whom he was describing. 'Aliens', he affectionately called them, with a knowing glimmer in his eyes. To be precise, Venusians. They had no body hair. They were supremely intelligent. And they had offered to share with the US government technologies which would benevolently eradicate famine, war, and disease.

Apparently the government aides asked for time to consider this offer. They came back to the gentlemen and declined it, saying that it would 'disrupt the economy too much'.

Frank began to show the slides.

It wasn't that I recalled these particular men. It was that ... I recognized their *features*. The ... 'shape of their faces'. And more profoundly, their *essence energy*.

I had 'awoken' to the Venusians. I remembered them. As a 'race', as a species similar yet distinctly different from us - from humans.[4] And I saw in them, a key. For Pedro - whom I'd awakened to only weeks before - I now recognized. He ... was a Venusian, too.

♥

Pedro.

My friend Mark, from the bookstore, suggested that we take a long weekend trip, rent a car, and drive to Mount Shasta. He'd been there. An amazing hike, he said. The air got thinner and thinner as you climbed. He'd never made it to the top. He felt it was time to try again.

We drove there, and camped. I began the ascent of the mountain with Mark, and felt a strong 'pull' to come down. Apparently, this wasn't why I came.

---

[4] Their civilizations are harmonious, highly intelligent, benevolent models of planetary culture. They live an 'ethic' of benevolence, like a race full of compassionate Boddhisatvas. Theirs is a society of Joy, of Love, of Peace.

Venusians can't be 'seen' by standard human technology, as they exist on a higher vibrational frequency than we do.

Jesus is said to have been of Venusian 'origin'.

I discretely waited out the weekend, conscious that I didn't want to sour Mark's evident delight in his hiking.

Early on our last morning, we packed our gear into the car and began to drive home.

Mark was in the front seat. I had a strong, emphatic sense to sit in the back. The reason why would soon evidence itself. I needed privacy - quiet, no conversation - to experience another trance.

As we drove - 'away' from the magnitude of Mount Shasta - Pedro came almost forcibly into my mind. I had known 'of' him. A dear friend of mine had raved about a concert he had given in Vancouver not long before.

Why was he presenting himself to me? It was as if ... I was supposed to 'notice him'. As if ... there was some significant connection between us. A connection which was beginning to *wake up.*

This was all quite mysterious to me, still, as we returned to Vancouver. Mark dropped me off at the friend's apartment where I was staying. I found myself, once in the quiet of her home, gravitating to her stereo. There, atop a stack of CD's, was one of Pedro's. I put it on.

It was like I was an innocent child, suddenly plunged into maturity. I flew toward the speakers, hugging my ears into them *so tightly.* I would have climbed inside, if I physically could have. What? What was he *saying?*

He was talking about the eagle. Flying into the Light. Just like with Alessandro's poetry which Shakey had decoded for me - and like his own recent 'First Folio' writings 'through' me - I could hear the deeper meanings of Pedro's words *on their many levels.*

I knew too, with acceptance and a wave of resignation throughout my entire being - like a mysterious sense of 'defeat' - that Pedro, like Alessandro, might not know himself exactly 'what' he was saying. Was he awake? If so, to what degree? Was I hearing something 'through' him, through his words? Or did he know it, too?

I was distinctly aware that I had no idea … 'why' I was remembering Pedro. Other than to feel less alone knowing that he, too, (at least on the level of consciousness of his lyrics) 'saw the vision'. Was there something that we were to do? I listened in for further guidance, and I was shown that, together, he and I would 're-create the forgotten language'. The language which we all - *all humans on this Earth* - had once spoken, yet had forgotten. An ancient, unifying language *which we all would speak again.*

♥

I had begun to gypsy a few weeks before. I had been given clear guidance to put my belongings into storage - and 'gypsy'. Stay with friends in my own familiar city. Trust that, step by step, I would have a 'home'.

I sensed very clearly that this was a preparation. That I would be 'moving continent'. I had no idea to where. Yet it made sense. To trust that my physical needs would always be cared for, here in my own city, would make it easier for me to trust, in a foreign land.

♥

I was staying at my friend Jason's by the time the conference calls began. One of the men I'd met at the Conclave of Michael passed through Vancouver on a business trip, and we had lunch. He was intrigued to hear more details of my 'vision', and he asked if he could tell a few people about them when he got home.

He apparently did, because the phone rang. He had a friend on the line with him, Casey, who was keen to speak with me. She had a few questions. I found myself in a mild trance, replying from a level beyond my thinking brain. At the end of the call, Casey asked if she could call again, and invite a few other people onto the line.

Over the course of several weeks, the conference calls grew. They became international. Environmental engineers, physicists, social change experts. All of them people on the leading edge of their fields. All of them keenly interested in and dedicated to awakening consciousness and the practicalities of healing our global wounds.

As the conference calls progressed, I would notice that - because on each call we would set a pre-determined time for the next - I would be drawn to lie down about half an hour before the phone was to ring. And I would fall asleep.

This would surprise me, initially, as 'I' would normally prepare myself by being 'awake' in order to have a bright mind. 'I' was clearly not the one doing the speaking on these calls, though. I was the voice. Something beyond me was the mind.

So I would fall asleep. And a gentle inner nudge would awaken me. Thirty seconds to a minute - just enough time to 'come to' - before the phone rang.

♥

My guides had told me, while in seclusion, that I would be a 'lucid channel'. That I wouldn't vacate my body in order to allow higher consciousnesses to speak through me. Unlike many other channels who - to varying degrees - 'vacate' their bodies, so that the entity communicating through them brings with it its own physical mannerisms and voice. No, I would stay present.

The reason for this was vital for me to understand. As my voice would remain 'mine'. And my body and the way it held itself and moved would remain 'me'. There would be nothing 'about me' that would alarm people when I channeled. I would be a physical, tangible, recognizable vehicle from higher consciousness to this incarnate plane. 'Like' humans, people could fearlessly engage with me, thus connecting themselves up to their *own* communication with the Divine. When I channeled I would be a momentary interface, a 'splice'.

♥

It was while I was staying at Jason's that I received the 'Second Installment of the Vision'. It took about three days to receive it. Much quicker than the seven and a half months of seclusion! - the 'wiring' phase and the foundational 'First Installment' reception - which together had prepared me so well for this.

It - the 'Second Installment of the Vision' - is elaborate, yet extraordinarily simple.

All *energy* which came into Time and Space - into 'form' - made its voyage through infinity in the shape of a Dove. A multi-dimensional 'Dove'.

Prior to Time, all energy existed as the Whole. As the Unified Field of Light. There was no duality, and thus no suffering. Suffering wasn't even a concept. In fact, there were no concepts. There was no 'thought', as we know thought. Light simply was. It was a state, thus an experience, of continuous bliss.

One day (language requires that this be told in 'Time'), some of this whole energy 'fell'. It slipped, something which had been entirely unprecedented.

Now, there were two states - the fully awake consciousness of the Whole, which was slightly less whole as a result of some of it 'falling'. And the forgetful consciousnesses - those who fell - who for simplicity I'll call the 'Greys'.[5] *The Greys had no memory of being of the Whole.* In falling, *they forgot their origin.*

This ... is how Time began. Those consciousnesses still within the fully awake state of the Whole - they could *see* this. They could understand it.

And they devised a plan.

Some of them ... would volunteer. Most of them ... would remain as the 'Whole', as an anchor for the plan.

---

[5] I first came into conscious awareness of the Greys as a race of beings who are 'etheric' relative to human perception. That is, they exist on a slightly higher vibrational frequency than our day-to-day senses can perceive. With more exposure and increasingly lucid awareness of the existence of the Greys and 'who they are', I came to realize that they have filtered through human consciousness to affect how we live and think – 'who we are'. Their influence is evidenced in the way we as a race have strayed from the Light – how we have fallen from our own

Those who volunteered would 'drop', energetically, beneath the vibration of the 'Greys'. They would then arc up, in a trajectory, just like a boomerang. In their upward arc, they would collect the Greys. And All would come Home.

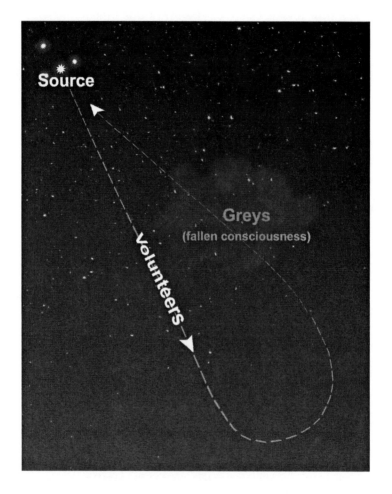

'the original, intended Volunteer trajectory'

---

awareness of ourselves as Divine Beings, as 'Children of God'. Again, 'As Above, So Below'.

In coming Home, the Greys would remember who they were. They would be able to see the fall (the 'past'). From the vantage of now being Home (part of the Whole again).

This was a brilliant plan.

However, as this circumstance had *never, ever arisen before,* it could not be foreseen what would happen as it was activated.

And so it transpired that, as the volunteers dropped - vibrationally, beneath the Greys - the Greys could then 'see' them. The volunteers came into their view.

Having forgotten themselves as being of the Wholeness - and thus not recognizing the volunteers, or who they were - they became frightened.

They sliced across the trajectory - the intended and natural *return 'arc'* of the 'boomerang' - *with a 'Veil'.*

They locked the volunteers in.

This, very basically, is the story of all of Time.[6] Its creation and perpetuation. Its 'why'.

---

[6] The 'Wheel of Time'. In the Wheel, souls can 'die' and rise to the soul plane, though they cannot transcend beyond it. *Unless they become more conscious than the Veil.*

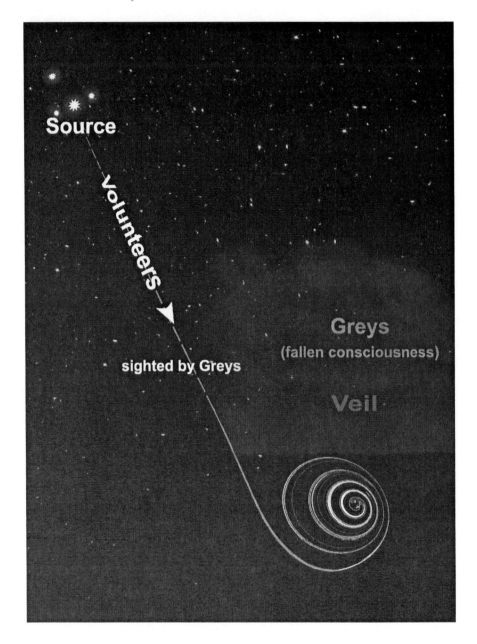

'the Veil locking the Volunteers in'

♥

Yet this is not all. There is a brilliant intelligence to this, if we will *wake up to see it - to remember it.*

The volunteers journeyed together, creating 'of themselves' their own vehicle. They traveled as **the Dove.**[7]

As they journeyed through what would become the far reaches of universes and galaxies, they knew to leave behind 'beads', breadcrumbs, berries to mark the path.

Beyond the eighth dimension, energy expands exponentially. Inwards. And outwards. Both become infinities.

As the Dove slowed its vibration, descending lower and lower, it entered into what became the 'linear' aspect of the cosmic birth canal. From here - the 8th dimension to the 3rd - there is a 'path'. Until very recently it has been like a 'connect-a-dot' path - out of alignment - yet linked by memory strings. A few 'light years' ago,[8] these dimensional markers *re-aligned.* The cosmic birth canal magnetically *reactivated.* Just as the uterus softens and expands when a woman is ready to give birth. Consciousness is actively being pulled through it, again.

---

[7] The Dove is Creation Theory *known* - recognized - in its full cosmic glory, power, and implications. Unlike 'Creation Theory', the Dove is in process - not yet complete. The most precious aspect of its design is still to come.

This - is the 'turning inside out'. When we begin to re-awaken to a sufficient degree, we realize that *the path is completely known to us.* It is simply the 'direction' that is new. For in returning 'Home', to Wholeness, we are flying 'in' along the path we once flew 'out'.

The 'markers' along this cosmic re-birth path are consciousnesses just like you and I. These are the dimensional 'gatekeepers'. They appear as gods to us from our vantage here on Earth (looking 'up'), only because they are that much more 'whole' than we are, here in form. They are that much more 'awake'.

♥

When the Dove, minus the consciousnesses who remained further out as the dimensional 'markers', 'flew in' - it flew in, it burst through An - the centre star in Orion's belt.

As it burst through, it fractured into waves, and the final splitting of soul from soul began to occur. Shards of consciousness were scattered, as if a bomb blast.[9] The pieces of a great puzzle were torn apart.

Waves of these consciousnesses made it 'in', intact.

---

[8] Time is quickening. Energetic 'arrival' in the 3D is swifter. Light years aren't their 'former duration' any more.

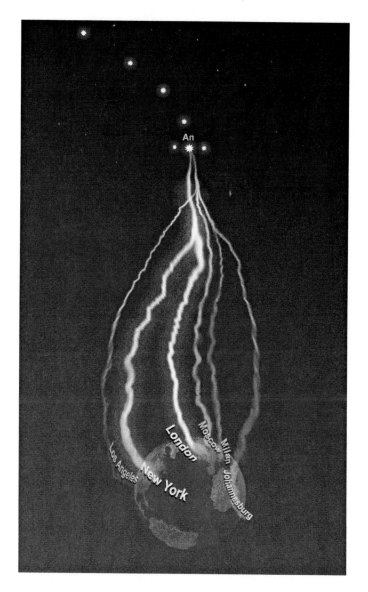

'the Waves landing energetically on the 'globe' ... through An'

---

[9] The 'Big Bang'. The 'Map' I was shown includes elements of the Creation, Big Bang, and Evolution theories which all are 'aspects' - angles of perception of the whole of what took (and is still taking) place.

The first wave of consciousness to fly in was the 'Beak' - of the 'Dove'. Just as in a airplane or a ship it is the pilot, that which steers the vessel. It 'landed', energetically, where London would become.[10]

The second wave was the 'anchors' - the anchor points mapping the entire bird. It touched down, energetically, in what would become New York City. This wave's 'mathematical formula' is 957 + 12 + 2. Nine hundred and sixty-nine souls, plus 2 'gatekeepers', as bridges - connectors to the next waves.

The third wave of the Dove's arrival - in what would eventually become 'Space and Time' - was four waves within a wave. These anchored near what would become Los Angeles, Johannesburg, Moscow, and Milan.

The next waves after waves were the various layers of the Dove, much like filigree layers of an onion, or a beautiful pastry, or a Russian doll.

I remembered all this. I regained my memory - of the 'sketch' of the entire Dove.

And I remembered, too, that as form evolved, these pieces scattered. The 'Big Bang' would reverberate, like a continuous explosion, throughout all of Time.

♥

---

[10] This was the beginning 'moment' of what would become 'Evolution Theory'.

Just like sliding a bead of ink between two glasses, one fitted inside the other, and the bead 'stretching' - *'Time' is reversed.* *Wholeness is regained* - by sliding the glasses into their original relationship. 'Unstretching the bead'. Returning it to peace.[11]

---

[11] In so doing, no trace - no memory - of the stretch remains.

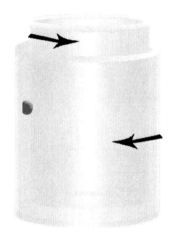

'the bead of ink 'stretching' between two fitted glasses
- it returns to its original state, without leaving a trace of its path!
… it 're-collects' itself … *in its entirety'*

The healing of the *Dove* is the same.

Awakening is augmented, logarithmically, as pieces of the Dove - the vehicle, the 'puzzle' - are reunited. Pockets of 'war' on planet Earth exist where there is the greatest chaos, the greatest confusion - pieces of the puzzle in the greatest disarray in relation to each other. Pockets of 'peace' on the planet exist where adjoining souls of the Dove - pieces of the puzzle - are either inter-connecting or are near to each other. Here there is stillness, harmony. Here … *memory is regained.*

The 'Second Installment of the Vision' which I received - it is this *Map.* The Map … of how this, the re-creation of the *Dove,* will take place.

♥

How it Happens

- Conclaves and Caravans

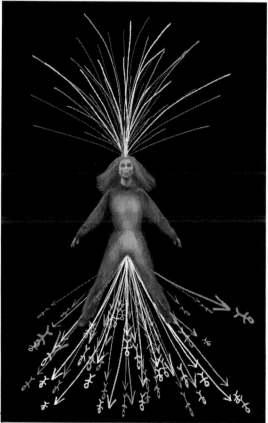

I remembered the Beak. I remembered them. All 48 + 2 of them.[1]

I remembered them as they 'flew through' me.

Energetically. They flew through my body.

I recognized them, because they had done this once before.

[1] The '2' are the gatekeepers of a wave - they are the 'bridge' between one wave and the next. In the case of the Beak, the '2' are present with the 48 during their awakening process, ensuring that no other energy enters this consciousness 'container' - that it is 'pure'. When the Beak is fully awake, the '2' are then free to awaken with their own - the next - wave. This principle of the 'process' is true with all of the waves.

'the Beak souls flying energetically through the author

in preparation for

the journey 'out' '

When the first wave - the wave of the Beak - flew in[2], Alessandro and I held the opening, An, as if the cervix of a womb.[3] And all the souls within our wave flew 'through' us.

---

[2] This was the moment of 'Bo' realis - in 'Anaqua Borealis' - the energy of the Dove exploding through the final portal into confined 'Creation'.

[3] Alessandro and I are of the first wave of the Dove - the 'Beak'.

**'the Beak souls flying through Allesandro and the author
at the portal of An**

on the way 'in' '

So my body, my energy being, was keenly able to remember them again - like articulately culling, sorting one's own ducklings from a massive flock.

It was an absolutely remarkable experience.

♥

I was taken through an 'experiential rehearsal' - an energetic experience of something before it manifests here, in the density of the physical world.   An 'experiential rehearsal' - of the first 'Conclave'.

When the Time is right. The souls of the Beak - the first wave - the forty-eight souls. Plus the two gatekeeper souls - the bridges to the next wave.

They will know to gather. They will 'hear the call'.

They will convene. And together, they will enter a collective trance.

In this trance, they will see the blueprint. They will remember the 'story'. They will remember the Dove.

They will release their bodily identity, in terms of purpose and personality. For the rest of Time, they will work together, to wake the others up.

It was shown to me like this.

'Horizontal Path (individuals) ... leading to
Inclined Path (individuals and small clusters) ... leading to
Vertical Path (original soul family 'waves' –
the Caravans arising from the Conclaves)

We have all been, to greater and greater degrees in recent time, led to work on 'projects'. Enlightenment projects. Life before this was 'horizontal'. These projects were the beginning of the 'inclined path'.

When we awaken in our soul clusters, during our own Conclave, we enter the collective, vertical path. Together, as an original wave of souls, we work in the only remaining project. The project of the collective awakening.

♥

As the Beak completes its Conclave, its two gatekeepers are released. The second wave - the New York wave - receives its call. They (the 957 + 12 + 2) gather for their Conclave, their collective awakening.

Then the Beak is released to begin its Caravan.

This pattern ripples ... each Conclave metamorphoses into its Caravan ... onward ... as waves of awakening ... until all of the waves have *remembered the Dove!*

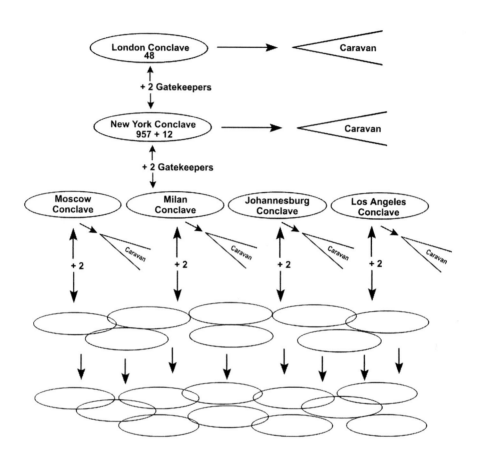

'the Conclaves and Caravans 'sequence' '

And when a certain degree of 'levity' is acquired. When enough waves have entered into this process to establish 'critical mass',[4] the Dove begins to lift off. We leave behind the 'density' of illusion. We become ultimately transparent. We shed the 'splits' of

---

[4] There is a distinct 'critical mass' for different stages of this process. The critical mass for the ascension of the Dove is a certain number of waves having entered into the mass awakening process - the Conclaves and the Caravans.

the left and right brain, the implants of the digestion, excretion, and procreation processes. We become free as Light Beings. We 'eat' Light, and Love, again.

♥

The Beak carries the consciousness of the *steering,* the guiding, just like the pilot of a jet.

The *whole* Dove - each and every piece of the puzzle, together - remembers the whole path. The whole Dove flew in. As a whole entity, it knows *through itself, viscerally,* where it made its 'turns'.

The whole Dove will reconvene. And in so doing it will reactivate its 'sonar'. Its 'radar'. Its directional intelligence. It will - we will - remember our collective path *'Home'.*

♥

Remembering my wave - the Beak - was unlike any experience I have ever known in form. It was a reunion - a reunion that pre-dates Time.

We had met together as souls before incarnating into this, the final lifetime. We gathered, under a large cosmic 'tree'.

It was a peaceful occasion, recalling and reviewing where we would meet, how we would recognize each other, and all the other details of our 'landmarks'. Our signposts for this upcoming lifetime.

We - our wave - met on Venus. It was our final stopover point before this incarnation.

The second wave - the 'New York wave' - stopped over on Sirius.

Each wave had its own, last stopover. Its own reconvening before incarnating in this completion lifetime.[5] Its own final opportunity to review its signposts, its meeting places, how they would recognize each other via *essence,* prior to falling asleep into this final birth.

♥

Remembering my wave was like the one reunion. I wait with patience for it to transpire in flesh, in Earth Time.

♥

I was shown the Conclave of the London Beak. I remembered it, energetically, like a 'preview'.

---

[5] In the soul plane, Time is not linear, though it overlays with linear Time as we are conditioned to perceiving it here on Earth.

Twenty four souls 'sit' - around an oval 'table'. And twenty four behind them. The two gatekeepers watch the 'door', ensuring that no energy attempts to enter to disrupt this. For these souls surrender into collective, awakening trance.

When they 'see' - when their collective memory of the blueprint is complete - they begin to remember their 'Caravan'.

The purpose of the Caravans is to ease the way for the next waves, each in their respective succession, to *hear their calls*. And to have sufficient inner power to overcome any resistance that would hold them back from gathering.

The swell of the Caravans will bring so much Memory onto this planet that fear will quickly lose its hold.

♥

All of this - the 'Second Installment of the Vision' - reminded me of the 'sling'.

In New York City, I had received one of the most potent visions of my life. It measured on the scale of the 'white rope ladder', and 'turning inside out' - visions and metaphors which would be shown to me time and time again.

One morning, in New York, my guides had asked me to take a walk to a playground. Shakey was particularly gentle with me -

and so I felt a palpable sense of trepidation that arose every time - before a 'big lesson' was about to be shown.

They, through him, asked me to sit on a swing.

I love swinging. It is one of my favorite, most liberating experiences. I feel like a perpetual child, a divine child when I'm on a swing.

This time it felt more serious.

I sat down, knowing in my bones that something was coming.

They showed me … this.

A sling, like a harness that would slip under a huge boat in order to lift it onto dry dock.

This sling … slowly descended from the skies. It came delicately, quietly, unnoticeably from the 'unseen' worlds, into this world, still unseen.

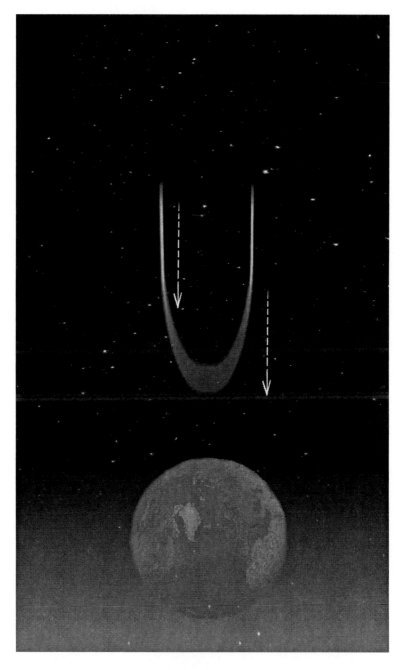

'the sling'

It touched down, softly, on the 'pavement'. Onto the human created world of civilization.

And it rested there awhile.

It rested there long enough for the people to become acclimatized to its presence. - I saw people walking on it, over it, and off of it again, as they went about their daily business, completely unaware of its presence.

And then ... as slowly and silently as it had landed ... it began to rise.

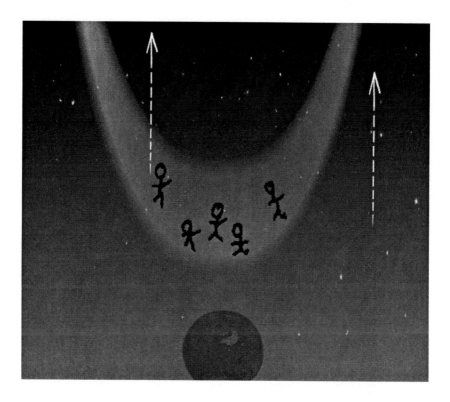

As it rose, it lifted all those sleeping people, gradually into higher consciousness. Effortlessly and painlessly, it lifted them - waking them *up*.

This reminded me of a 'poem' which came to me around this time.

'knocking their heads
... against a soft pillow'

A metaphor … for waking people gently *up*.

♥

I remembered a few things then.

The image - of the teeter totter.   An explanation of critical mass.

'the teeter totter of critical mass'

That … at a certain point, enough people will have awakened to a great enough degree that … the fulcrum point will shift. And all of incarnate consciousness will 'glide'. Glide into awakening … as the teeter totter shifts.

♥

Critical mass - that required to begin the visible, tangible activation of this 'Map' - my guides told me over and over again, is *only twenty four people.* Twenty four souls, incarnate, fully awake to the 'plan'. To the big picture. Fully awakened from the 'dream', the collective 'spell'.

Twenty four souls, incarnate, who have fully pierced the Veil.

It was only recently that I could see the correlation of this - with the *twenty four souls sitting around the oval table.*

I had sensed, all along, that this was a 'particular … twenty four souls'. That they were currently scattered somewhat around the globe. That most of them didn't know each other, yet.

That soon … in 'soon Time' … *they would.*

♥

Early in seclusion, I was given the year '2012'.[6] This was the year, I was told, that the Beak would begin to lift up.

I am personally grateful that, as of several years ago, my guides have pulled 'dates' out of my visions. This part of the visions I always felt stress around. Without the 'dates', I can see the visions with ease.

And so I know, now, that this process will unfold in its own Time. My current sense is that 2012 will be a 'guideline date'. Whatever is 'complete' by 2012 will be complete. Whatever is prepared, will be prepared.

Time will tell!

♥

---

[6] This is a significant year according to the Mayan calendar, the mathematical architecture of the Great Pyramids, Solara's writings, and apparently numerous other sacred sources. I knew only of Solara's writings at the time I was in seclusion.

In seclusion, a frequent symbol I was shown was the 'Q'.

A spiral of energy, 'unwinding' counterclockwise.

And on a particular circle around, it would *shoot off, like an arrow. On a 'new' trajectory.*

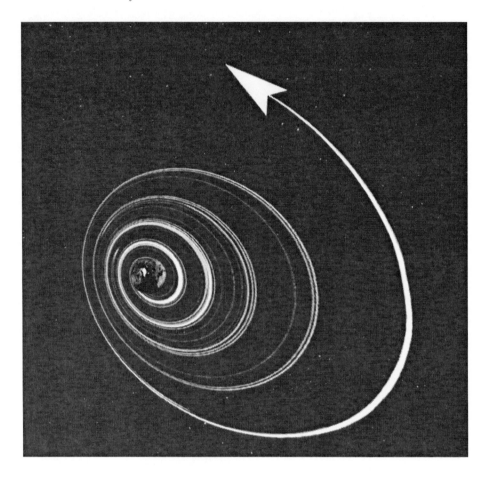

'the 'Q' exiting the Wheel of Time in the 'boomerang trajectory' '

Out and around and up, to the left.

This precisely coincided with the 'arc' I was shown. The arc of the volunteer souls. They had descended from ... 'up, left'. They arced down. Curved, at the bottom of the arc. And, on their early ascent, they were blocked off ... by the 'Veil'. Their momentum had no choice but to circle around, over and over again - as the creation of 'Time'.

Now - soon - this same energy would regain its *clarity of its original momentum*. It would leave the 'circle', the 'Wheel of Time'. It would begin its final arc … of the **original boomerang**.

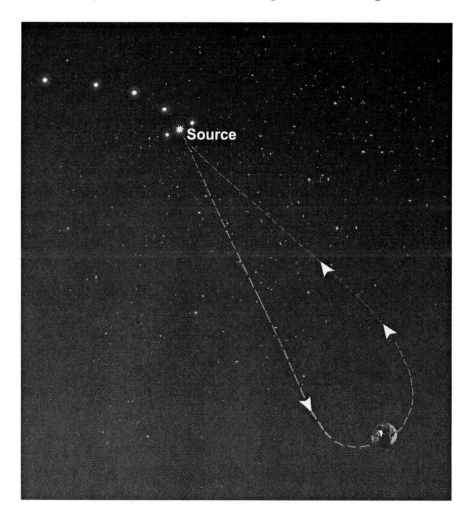

'the original Volunteer trajectory'

♥

There was also the image, the metaphor, of the Jack-in-a-Box.

My guides explained to me, showing me through this image, that 'Time' has been the oppressive *downward pressure of denial, of forgetfulness.* It has pressed 'Jack' - the volunteers, the awake consciousnesses - into the 'box'.

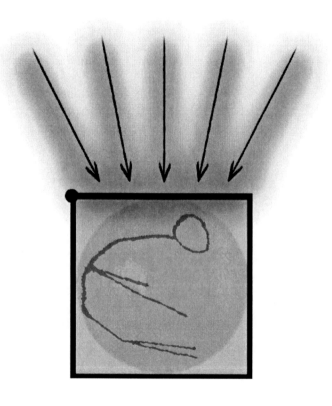

They showed me how much 'force' is spent to keep the power of consciousness repressed, 'contained'.

When enough power of awakening memory builds up in 'Jack', the lid of the box will explode off.

' 'Jack' exploding beyond the lid of the 'box' (the Veil) ... free to fly again!'

This will be the moment (envisage an overlaying of images) when the original trajectory - the 'tag' on the 'Q' - will be free again.

The lid will be off. And Jack - *all consciousnesses captive in 'Time'* - will be free to fly.

♥

There was another important aspect to the 'Second Installment of the Vision'. It was the remembering of the Triads. And the Triad Trilogies.

It blew me away - how masterful my guides were at orchestrating my awakening. How had they kept Alessandro, absolutely completely, out of my present awareness while they awakened me to Pedro?

If they hadn't, my memory of the three of us would have effected the 'reactivation of our combined energy' - ahead of its Time.[7]

I remembered the principle of Triads *through remembering having been in one.*

I physically remembered, in the energy of my body, having … 'been in a body, with two other souls'.

---

[7] Soul groupings are like energy chemistry - certain soul clusters 'create' or impel certain effects of mass awakening.

As I remembered into this more deeply, I recognized. *That I had been the Mind. That Alessandro had been the Heart / Speech. And that Pedro had been the Body.* I would gradually, and with much more detail a few years later, come to recognize that I was an incarnation - a strand - of the Archangel Michael energy. Alessandro was an embodiment of Uriel. And Pedro of Archangel Gabriel.

With this new element as a foundational basis, I could then understand when my guides began to outline human history *from the viewpoint of Triads, and Triad Trilogies.*

In all major turning points in history, the 'agent' of major transformation has been a Triad or a Triad Trilogy.

Three souls, in one.[8] Or three souls, in each of three beings.[9]

Gandhi. Shakespeare. Jesus. Buddha. Mohammed. Hitler. Alexander the Great. Joan of Arc. And so many others.

In order to *turn the plot,* just like in a play, a *more potent energy had to incarnate.*

A single soul would have been too easily swayed by the 'mind controlling' - by the beliefs of the time. A 'stronger entity' would be needed, to 'shift the plot'. To shift the current thinking and thus acting of the day.

---

[8] A triad.
[9] A Triad Trilogy.

When a particularly large shift was needed, a Triad Trilogy was created. Nine souls were chosen. Three incarnated in the 'active Triad' - the one which would be visible, and which would carry the character's name.

The other six souls would incarnate in two other people, often geographically distant, like 'ballast'. They would be 'anonymous', seldom identifiable or known to the active Triad in any visible way. These were called the 'passive Triads'.

This made so much sense to me.

In a single soul being, like you and I, we embody the three functions of Mind, Heart / Speech, and Body. How often do you meet someone - or have a fleeting experience of - all three aspects of yourself being completely aligned? In most people, most of the time, these three internal aspects are in discord.

Leadership - true leadership - my guides showed me, exists when a person's Mind, Heart / Speech, and Body are completely congruent. Then they are completely honest, because they are completely transparent. They are not hiding anything. There is no 'inner war'.[10]

---

[10] This had been the intended 'design' of Jesus' lifetime - to, over the course of His long life, exemplify and thus 're-wire' *in the incarnate human design* - the completely congruent, balanced relationship of mind, heart/speech, and body. For this is the model of God. Jesus' lifetime was intended to be the 'creation period' in which humanity would come to directly mirror God *in its incarnate existence.*

So I remembered that Alessandro, Pedro and I had been a Triad.[11]

Somehow, the memory of this had to do ... with the all important Beak waking up.

♥

In a Triad, the Gabriel consciousness acquiesces itself to a 'pre-conscious state'. Meaning that it becomes the energy 'base' into which the Uriel and the Michael consciousnesses or souls are anchored. Just like a lotion, in which the fragrance droplets permeate.

Gabriel was the 'host'.

Michael's function was to 'steer the being'. To be its umbilical cord. To connect it - *always* - to the guidance of the higher Light. Like Shakey and my other guides did for me. It was Michael's role to be a constant connection to more awake consciousness. To ensure that the incarnate being always heard and

---

[11] I recognize fully that Alessandro, Pedro and/or myself may be 'stand ins' - not the 'actual souls' who were in the Triad I was remembering. In the awakening of planetary consciousness, there are times when a soul is called to 'stand in' for another soul - to play the part of *preparing*. Preparing for the larger event. Stand ins can be more suitable - more able to do this 'preparation' - as they aren't in the full heat of the 'real role'. Just like in movies and stage productions, when another actor 'stands in' for a lead player until the actual filming or live performance takes place.

And so we may simply be preparing the way for the reactivation of other souls.

followed the guidance of its guides - the 'Birds' Eye View' - the vantage from which the Earthly 'play' could be wholly viewed.

Uriel's function was to communicate with the people. Uriel was the incarnate being's 'voice'.[12]

This was the configuration, in each and every Triad which existed.

It always was the same.

♥

We are all single souls now. Every person who has incarnated in recent times is a single soul within their body. There are no Triads currently on the planet, nor will there be, again.

Why?

Because in this awakening time, we must *all be free to choose.*

Being in a Triad is not an easy experience. For the Gabriel consciousness must not disagree. And the Michael consciousness must receive and distribute the guidance, at all cost. And the Uriel consciousness must be the agent of communication, no matter the message.

I have no attachment to the three of us reconvening *in awakened memory of a Triad.* If I am simply to 'pave the way', so be it.
[12] Gabriel's grounding and Michael's steering roles enabled this 'voice' *to be received on Earth.*

In coming into being in a Triad - every time this occurred in the great play's 'design' - each of the three souls needed to agree *not to disagree*. They needed to surrender to the wisdom of each other's roles.

In understanding this, I was ready to comprehend the fallacy of 'free will'. My guides described this as the greatest misnomer in the human language.

What most people think of as 'free will' is 'doing whatever I please'.

True Free Will is being in alignment with God, with one's higher self. It is the absolute alignment of the 'little self' - the little brother or little sister, the incarnate aspect of the being - with the 'bigger self'. The more omni-conscious Self.

'Listening in' - following our intuition, our discerned guidance - *aligns us with our Higher Self.*

So Now, here on this planet, in this time of ultimate choice, we need to be free, each and every one of us, to choose. Without being bound in agreement to 'not disagree' with our Triad souls.

This partly explains why the planetary population is booming. 'Each one in a singular body'.

♥

The most important principle of the mass awakening, my guides told me frequently, reiterating it at every stage of my own awakening journey, is that *all energy is included.* No energy is left out.

All energy is included. The mass awakening is *completely inclusive.*

No energy is left out.[13]

♥

The Dove is the energetic 'vehicle' ... created of all energy which ever incarnated here on Earth.

Imagine the Dove ... beautiful, full, white ... viewing it from above. Looking down ... toward it ... from the 'Birds' Eye View', the vantage of all fully awakened consciousness ... as if looking 'down' on the planet and all created form. The Dove ... its Beak stretched out, so that the farthest most tip of the bird is the tip of the Beak. And its feet stretched back, so that the farthest most tip of the bird is the tip of the toenails. And the wings stretched out and back, streamlined, gliding 'up'.

---

[13] There is no punishment, no retribution at this ultimate turning of *Time.* All energy which originated from Source (which is all there *is)* returns to Source. There is nothing 'outside' of this. - This is the ultimate 'turning inside out'. When it is complete, no dual states remaining, the 'outside and the inside are no more'. There will no longer be a distinction between them. All will be, again, *'Just Is'.* We will have traveled *Home* ... beyond duality ... through the *cosmic birth canal.*

'aerial view of the Dove'

The Dove is overlays of energy, woven intricately together, perfectly inter-feathered, latticed like a dimensional jigsaw puzzle.

Close your eyes for a moment. Feel inward. *Remember.*

...

Where are *you?* Where is your perfect place ... on the Dove?

What wave are you in?

♥

Sequencing. The collective awakening is all about *sequencing.* The perfect, filigree awakening, layer by layer, of consciousness ... of *Light.*

The consummate orchestration ... of the awakening 'Map'.

♥

When my guides had completed their transmission of the 'Second Installment of the Vision' to me, and they were sure that I had received it successfully, they let me know this.

That it hadn't been transmitted - this 'Map', this blueprint - in this way - to Earth, before.[14]

Before I asked why, they explained this to me ... If it was disclosed to human consciousness too soon, and it was in any way misperceived, misrepresented or in any way tainted, it would take *so much energy to purify it, again.* That, to 'lift it out', and make it intact again - for only in a pure, intact form could it be trusted ... This would take years. It had been two thousand years since the last attempt.

This 'Map', like so many other ancient wisdoms having suddenly begun to be released in recent years into collective consciousness. Now being shared, as their human 'vehicles' are urged through visions and prophecies that 'this is the Time'.

I know that, if this version of this book is received into human hands, now, 'it is the Time'.

---

[14] The Jesus lifetime was intended to be the delivery of the 'Map' to Earth - as well as its activation. More on this later.

England Calls

I knew it was Time to go to England - London, to be precise. It was Time to 'call' ... the London Beak.

Many of the people on the conference calls were of the Beak. It turned out that, via connections - so and so knows so and so knows so and so - all of the Beak were, eventually, linked to someone in this group.

Yet it wasn't like sending out invitations. Because this was not to be a gathering 'on Earth'. It was to be a journey into deep trance, to awaken *collective memory*. And *only if the Time was precisely right,*[1] would the 48 + 2 *know to come.*

---

[1] In this mass awakening, each individual and the collective waves can only awaken to the degree that the *whole will allow.* Fear and unreadiness on anyone's part 'puts on the brakes', slowing the process down. For awakening has a powerful ripple effect. Each tiny degree of awakening consciousness effectively sets the entire mobile into motion, triggering - inviting, calling - the awakening, *the remembering,* of all Truth. For nothing is 'separate'. *All is interconnected.*

This critical principle allows us to grasp why Christ was crucified. Not all energy was ready. And so 'he', the vehicle, the catalyst for the ultimate awakening, was blocked from fulfilling his task - of awakening incarnate consciousness to its memory of itself *as the Light.* He and his life were designed to gradually - in the course of one lifetime - dissolve the *Veil* from the

I had personally heard several calls already in my life - 'calls' from the Higher Self, the unmanifest consciousness, the 'Great Soul' - to my 'little' self, my incarnate heart / body / mind. Jacob's Pillow, seclusion, the Earth Summit. I had followed these calls to places I'd never been, without research, completely through trust.

So if the London Beak Conclave was to take place now, I could only trust that my fellow souls of the Beak would hear this, their call, and follow it.

I gave away most of my belongings. I left the continent of my birth in this lifetime. And I flew.

♥

I was greeted by two people who'd also been at the Conclave of Michael in Banff. They had 'checked me out' (!) with a renowned London psychic since that time and had deemed me to be 'clear'. To be completely benevolent and accurate in what I was receiving. They had eventually found their way onto the conference calls, too. And they had 'flown through me', identifying themselves as being of the 48 + 2.

I stayed with them in a houseboat on the Thames.

---

consciousness of 'men'. He was meant to 'lift the lid' - *so that we would fly free again.*

It has been two thousand years of 're-design' since then. And now … here is the 'Map'.

Gradually, over the next few days, several key people from the New York wave appeared.

My guides had brought me into a clear understanding of 'stand ins'.

"All the world's a stage", Shake speare once said. This, a major turning point in the global 'script', was no exception.

They made it clear to me that, in the actual Conclaves, and in every stage of the collective awakening following that, *there would be no stand ins*. From that point on, every soul must take its original place in the 'Dove'. The only way that the collective memory ... the memory of the 'course', the path back 'Home' ... could be accurately remembered, was if *everyone was in their original place*. Memory, of such energetic things as this, is stored in the cells' intelligence within our 'body'. Just as our emotions and memories of this lifetime are recorded. They are encoded, neurologically, in our *body*.

They began to tell me that ... we evidently were slightly 'premature'. That ... just as Shakey had asked me to 'let go control', before I was ready ... this ... this *call* of the first Conclave - *it needed to take place now*. That the planet and its people weren't entirely ready *was not a thing to be upset about*. **The calling would trigger the awakening** - the awakening necessary for the *successful, later call*.

All of this happened so fast, I had no time for emotional reactions (dwelling in what was now past). I was swept, moment to moment, into the continuous present.

And so several incarnate souls would stand in for several London Beak souls[2] who would not *yet* appear. Not yet. Because the collective was not, quite, ready to allow this.

I did feel sadness. In order to call the Beak - and to come this far - I had had to trust with no error of doubt in the visions I was shown. Several times already it had been like walking a fine, delicate tightrope - absolutely no margin for error - with an ultimate void all around.

I had discerned every one of my visions for benevolence. And as they had all proved themselves as 'clear', I had no choice but to trust them completely.

If I doubted - how could I assist others to awaken?

The London Beak 'rehearsal' Conclave took place - at Raven's Ait[3], a small island on the Thames used mostly by rowing teams. For four days, we had the island to ourselves.

---

[2] The 'mathematical formula' of the number of souls in each wave refers to incarnate souls. Disincarnate souls - on the 'soul plane', the phase between lifetimes - are also linked in to these waves. As is all other energy present in the realm of Space and Time - geographies, plant and animal species, etcetera. The incarnate souls *represent* these. They anchor them. To understand this is quite elaborate. I'll leave this as a simple clarification for now.
[3] Several of those present felt keenly compelled to research the significance of this place. They found an ancient map with an energetic Dove overlayed over England. *Its Beak lay precisely over Raven's Ait.*

It was a rich and fascinating passage. Those present were among the most brilliant thinkers of our Time - thinkers with heart, dedicated to finding and developing solutions to Earth's and humanity's great crises.

Yet it was more of a 'sharing' - a sharing of technologies and possibilities - than it was the 'Conclave' that I was shown will, at precisely the right Time, take place.

For, in order for the London Beak Conclave to occur in form, the precise 48 + 2 souls who originally flew in in that wave must convene. And they - and planetary and universal consciousness - must be ready. Ready for them to enter into collective trance. Ready for them to awake.

Timing is everything. Readiness is all.

We are all linked, invisibly. The 'collective unconscious' which Jung identified is real. Like a massive, intricate mobile, we only allow others to awaken at the pace that we are ready. Otherwise we intervene. We put on 'invisible brakes'. We set up invisible barriers. We block the awakening. We block the truth.

So I understood - that in order for my fellow Beak souls to hear the call and gather - for the first time in incarnate flesh *since before the beginning of Time* - all energy would need to be ready for this. All energy would need to 'step aside', and allow it *to begin.*[4]

---

[4] There are several key 'turning points' - moments of 'critical mass' - in the mass awakening, each with intricate stages leading them to the next. Within the context of the 'Map', the next 'turning point' which will occur in our Earthly experience

♥

The Conclave 'rehearsal' was complete. The others present were stimulated and inspired by the discussions which had taken place. None of them, it seemed, really understood what I meant by 'collective trance'. Or 'remembering'.

I was saddened that it hadn't yet been Time. I was saddened that the first principle of my 'vision' wasn't yet understood. I had no choice but to be patient. When all was ready, the 48 + 2 would know. And perhaps they alone would understand what I meant by 'collective trance'.

♥

Those present at the 'rehearsal' Conclave returned to the geographic locations from which they'd come. Except for the key New York wave people who, intriguingly, understood more clearly

---

will be the convening of the London Beak. The next 'turning point' will be when the London and New York waves have completed their Conclaves. The re-awakening of the Dove will then be secured. The third turning point in our 'future view' will be the 'lift off' of the Dove - just like a jet (metaphysically), its Beak (its pilots' cockpit) ascending into flight.

than the Beak people who'd been present, what it was that 'I' set out to do.[5]

To an outside onlooker it might have appeared that we were finished for the time. Yet guidance was clear. Even though it wasn't precisely Time yet for the Beak to recreate itself - its 48 + 2 souls *coming together*[6] - just like in American football, there was more 'yardage' to be gained before I could rest.

At this point in my awakening 'journey', my guides explained one of the most important principles to me. That ... disincarnate entities not only cannot intervene without invitation, *they cannot see all.* Not all of them have been incarnate - not all of them know the thick dynamics of Earth existence. And, most importantly, none of them are *incarnate now.* They can, with considerable exactness, ascertain what humanity is ready for *from their vantage.* Yet, without 'checking it out', they cannot know for sure.

And so, they explained to me, at the time of their calling the London Conclave together 'through' me - *it looked from their vantage as if all energy might have been ready.* The only way to know for sure was to try. It was close. Yet not *quite* ready then.

And so ... they entered into a most fascinating process of ascertaining what wasn't ready. And *how to assist it to be so.*

---

[5] Remember that when the pieces are scattered there is chaos, confusion. Without the whole of the Beak present, some of the souls were blind. It was as if they couldn't see, couldn't hear. As if their collective eyes and ears were missing.

[6] Like 'humpty dumpty', the scattered pieces rejoined.

This was one of the most amazing moments in my entire seclusion experience. Witnessing disincarnate consciousnesses witness us.

They realized that there was one thing, *in the brilliant orchestration and timing of their rescue plan* - their plan of how to jumpstart the 'original trajectory ... of the volunteers' - which they didn't anticipate. One, vital, thing.

They never, ever imagined that ... humanity would have become *so fossilized.* That *when the lid was lifted from the cage. We would not notice it.*

Like fish that keep swimming on one side of a tank when a former barrier has been removed. Or birds which remain in a cage when a door is opened.

They never imagined. That - when, after all of Time, the 'lid' was lifted - the *Veil dissolved.* **That humanity would not notice this.**

Back to the drawing board, in a sense. To figure out how to de-fossilize the human mind.

♥

So this - was what the next phase of my life was about.

I, and several colleagues with me (all of the New York wave) worked together in a most inspiring way. Together we were led on the next phase of this adventure.

First, in England, we were guided to endeavor to link with Alessandro. To ascertain whether he was blocked from 'hearing' the call. It was clear that he was.

So we were led to India. To meet the Dalai Lama.

We were staying in a small town in rural England at the time - a quieter place to be than London. Shaftsbury.

There was a vibrant festival taking place that evening.

I was guided to leave my colleagues and wander 'alone' amidst the crowd. Gentle guidance led me up a hill, weaving graciously through the throngs of people. There I came to a spot, a clearing amidst the masses. Here I was to sit down.

It was noisy, joyous, raucous all around me. Suddenly it went silent. Inside of me, there was a silenced din.

I saw it then. I was shown it clearly.

The Dalai Lama, in his maroon and saffron robes. With his left arm outstretched, like a great wing.[7]

---

[7] As with the vision of Alessandro and I onstage, 'speaking', with he on the left and me on the right - in this vision, His Holiness was the active one, the interface with humanity. Alessandro was the passive one, the one being sheltered, the one in deepest communion trance.

In my memory with God prior to incarnating in this lifetime, God was on the left, me on the right. I was the one about to interface with humanity. God was anchoring me. (As He / She does when each soul incarnates.)

And there, in the cocoon-like shelter of his arm, cradled peacefully, was Alessandro.

I was told in those moments that the Dalai Lama was the only being alive on the planet who could hold the consciousness - the truth - into which Alessandro could awaken. He was the only being who could 'hold this space'. For Alessandro had developed a very public life. A very visible one. And to publicly reveal that he was 'led by inner voices' ... this was calling of him a huge hurdle, a huge leap of faith.

The Dalai Lama - for he *lived* this depth of sacred knowing, he was 'wired' to it, able to withstand daily this intense voltage of *Light,* of awakened, knowing consciousness - he could hold the space for Alessandro to awaken into it, and live it, too.

In this vision, I witnessed Alessandro's relief. His relief at finally being able to release the illusion. And his 'necessary adherence to it'. And the relief of it being Time, Time for him to *lead the truth.*

Before this vision was complete, I saw myself passing a white envelope to His Holiness. Without opening it, he knew its contents. The message within was simply ... 'It is Time'.

He knew his role. He was to set sacred steps of energy into motion.

♥

The next morning, when I shared this vision with my colleagues, Agni - one of my most potent 'colleagues' who, like all the others, simply appeared as if on cue at the perfect moment in my accelerated journey - burst out. "I'm the one. I know I'm the one. To find him. To find the Dalai Lama."

And so she went. She went to India, following him to the oasis of the Kalachakra, an initiation which His Holiness had very recently begun to hold with unprecedented frequency. The Kalachakra - the Tibetan Buddhist *initiation of mass enlightenment.*

Agni followed His Holiness into a remote region of northern India. Here she was blocked, blocked by one of his private secretaries. We had experienced this with Alessandro. The 'body guards', set in place to weed out unnecessary intrusions, weren't at a level of consciousness to recognize 'this'. They couldn't understand what it was that we were asking. And so, they simply ruled it out.

Agni followed her own, powerful inner guidance. She returned to Dharamsala, winter home of His Holiness and also to many Lamas and Rinpoches, His Holiness' advisors and teachers. Spirit led her, through an intricate maze, as if in a fantasy tale.

This Rinpoche told her to meet with that one, and that one insisted she meet the next. Finally, in meeting Khamtrul Rinpoche, one of His Holiness' closest advisors, he urged Agni. "Go to see the leaders of the four Tibetan Buddhist sects. His Holiness will ask you to do this anyway. Save time. See them first. For what you speak is true. They will recognize this. And they will stand behind you. Go. Go now."

And she did.

She was screened, interrogated in a great hall in front of two thousand monks of the Sakya 'PhD debating' lineage. Rigorously cross-examined by the Sakya head. She nearly broke down into tears, though she steeled herself in their presence. She knew that he was trying to break her - to see if in fact she spoke the truth.

She did. She passed. "Go to His Holiness", he said.

She sat before the head of the Nyingma lineage for several audiences[8] while he 'slept'. She traveled through a human war zone to find him.

Each time after the allocated hour, she left, knowing that she would return as many times as was necessary. Knowing without a doubt, that ultimately he would awaken to her.

Which he did. After many visits of silence - and him apparently 'sleeping' - he greeted her, awake with an enormous grin. He laughed. He said nothing. He simply laughed.

They laughed euphorically together. She was swept with relief, knowing that her determination and her trust had been recognized. She knew he 'saw' her.

---

[8] In Tibetan Buddhism, a meeting with a Lama or a Rinpoche - a spiritual teacher - is called an 'audience'.

"Go to His Holiness'" he said. "Tell him I have given you my blessing." And, as she was about to leave, he added. "There is no need for you to see the other Lamas. This is enough."

He intuitively knew, without her having shared this with either him or his aides, that Khamtrul Rinpoche had sent her - to meet the *four* heads - the heads of each of the four Tibetan sects. According to this, the Nyingma master, she had already passed the entire test.

She had passed the test, truly, because these great spiritual masters could read her energy. They could 'see' her - the consciousness which she carried.

On a more descriptive level, they recognized that she, and I, 'knew' things. Sacred knowledge described in deep and ancient Tibetan teachings. Teachings which lay people were not given access to. Teachings which we must have brought in with us, from *another life*.

In short, they recognized the sacred wisdom which we carried. Amongst it, knowledge of the Triads, and the Triad Trilogies. Principles that we couldn't possibly have known from our western upbringings.

♥

Agni returned to Dharamsala, triumphant that she had come so far, yet knowing we were still midway through the gauntlet. She was finally given access to Tenzin Geyche, a much more gentle and accessible private secretary to His Holiness.

She called. We had awaited her phonecalls with eager anticipation in the quiet stillness of rural England for *two weeks* - like loyal dogs with baited breath. What news?

"You must come", she said. "To trust us, they must meet you, too."

With that, my parents and I and one other colleague were on our way to India.

♥

Agni had everything prepared for us. We stayed at Tse Chok Ling monastery headed by Lama Thupten, one of the Lamas she had been intriguingly, rather mysteriously guided to meet.

Soon after our arrival we sat with Lama Thupten in private audience. He asked me to relate to him the nature of my visions.

I was barely through the preliminaries in recounting them, briefly, when he said, "Go to His Holiness. He must hear this." Then he added. "Meet with Denma Locho Rinpoche. He will clear the way for you."

My father witnessed this exchange with amazement. His daughter, whose incredulous journey he had beheld for several years, had just been greeted and welcomed by someone who 'understood' her - just like that - virtually without explanation.

Welcome to Tibetan life. And to India. Land of the holy people. To many in this culture, the spiritual, the 'invisible', is more real than real.

Lama Thupten asked my father, "In Canada, what do you do?" When he explained that he was a psychiatrist, Lama Thupten broke into respectful laughter. "You'd be out of work, here!" It was true. Despite the physical torture and psychological ordeal of fleeing their homeland in exile, all of the Tibetans we met were the most smiley, happy, jovial of people. Their culture was able to balance great hardship. They were a striking example of mind and heart health.

♥

Denma Locho Rinpoche. We met him in private audience in his home in the Green Hotel. He had an air of both warmth and seriousness about him.

He asked if I could 'write my visions down'. He would much appreciate this, he said. He would review what I'd written, and at his first opportunity, he personally would speak with His Holiness.

We returned to Tse Chok Ling. In the simplicity of my monastery room, I began this daunting task. Of reducing my visions to a few pages, hand typed on an ancient Indian typewriter, to be read by great Lamas for whom English was a second language.

The writing was intense, as it always is. I 'listened'. And after many hours, it was complete. I had the document which Denma Locho Rinpoche had requested.

We met with him again. He graciously received it. "At my first opportunity", he said.

We later learned that Lamas, even of his stature, cannot request an audience with His Holiness. That all requests must originate from His Holiness himself. All that Denma Locho Rinpoche could do was, like us, wait. When His Holiness called him, he and we together could make our next move.

My parents and I returned to Canada to 'rest'. Lama Thupten had suggested this. "It will likely take about two weeks", he said. Unexpectedly, Denma Locho Rinpoche fell ill. It took several months.

We received the call. Tenzin Geyche. Asking when we could return to India. To meet with His Holiness.

♥

We flew in time to acclimatize for two days before the meeting. It was one of the most intense few days of my life - like the potency of all of seclusion, compressed.

I sat on my monastery bed, motionless, as my third eye prepared itself. I knew. His Holiness and I would barely speak words. We would - like I had experienced once, in seclusion - communicate in 'third eye ping pong'.

The day arrived. We walked in silence through the rhododendron forest connecting his monastery with ours.

After being respectfully frisked (the Tibetan body guards carry no evident weapons - their psychic awareness seems to suffice), we waited briefly in an ante room. Then we were invited in.

We had an hour scheduled for our 'meeting'. An hour for two beings who had never met in flesh to discuss visions of the awakening of the universe.

And on top of that, we had another agenda to discuss first. In order to pass by his 3D 'guards', we had presented a 3D purpose. And so we were granted this precious audience in order to present His Holiness personally with a prototype of my father's brilliant 'invention'.

Dad had dedicated his soul and passion for two decades to the evolution in his consciousness of an 'idea'. Exploring the fundamental principles of how humans hear he had, through his own guidance, 'circumvented the brain's sound filters'. He had developed technology for recording and replaying sound *as it is*. Intact in its directionality, relativity in space, and amplitude and - especially exciting to me, *its frequency spectrum*. I ardently recognized it as a 'vehicle', a tool for 're-inflating human perception', expanding both our range of sound frequency reception and our brain's ability to decode it. Simply put, this is a tool for re-awakening human consciousness.

Dad's discovery passed His Holiness' 'guards' scrutinous tests. His Holiness has precious time available for private audiences.

So there we were, His Holiness keen to receive a tool which could aid him in more effectively transmitting his public teachings. And, as he so loves to tinker with things 'mechanical', his very own prototype for personal use.

It was nearing the end of our pre-determined 'hour'. And, miraculously, like the heaven's parting to reveal rays of streaming light, it happened. Like an invisible splice, somehow orchestrated, the conversation opened.

We had ten minutes left to discuss my visions. It was clear to him, that we would need more time. And so a second audience was scheduled, two days later. I would finally have my opportunity - to manifest this stage of my 'mission', in the flesh. The 'white envelope' as I'd seen it - it would be passed - to His Holiness.

Our next audience was like a 'business meeting' - cordial, yet direct.

He asked a question. I would barely be into the first phrase of my channeled response, when he asked the next. He had already perceived it - he had already 'received' it.

Our conversation was rapid, economic, intense.

At the end of this second meeting he had what he needed. He offered that - once Alessandro and Pedro and I had met - he would 'do all that he could to gather the rest'. He would offer his connections to assist ... ultimately uniting the 'Beak' of the Dove.

In parting he said, somewhat forlorn, "I'm not sure that the human family has the *Will*[9] for this", intoning their lack of discipline, of commitment - their 'ignorance' as the Tibetans so straightforwardly name it.

"I have Will. I have so much Will I barely know what to do with it!" I exclaimed. He grinned. Perhaps this is why I was given this 'task' - to remember the 'Map' *and to deliver it.*

We had made such headway. Yet ... The first step was still before us. The timing. The 'collective agreement' to the timing.

---

[9] My guidance had told me, just before entering seclusion at Beth's cabin, that *"Love is naught, without the guidance of the Will".* It doesn't matter how much Love we have awakened to. Without the Will to guide it it is weak, lame, mute. The two *together are what create the activation* - the combustion of *Light.*

Energetically, psychically, Alessandro, Pedro and I would need to be allowed to meet.[10]

♥

A few days later, at a small house on a Himalayan hillside which my parents were renting, I felt a sudden, intense wave of fatigue. Within moments they departed for a hillside walk. And I was alone.

I had come to recognize this fatigue. It was a signal - a signal asking me to 'become still. And listen in.'

That I did.

I lay on a bed, restful, motionless.

I was shown the energetic linking, like brothers of a similar energy. Of His Holiness and Alessandro. And of Khamtrul Rinpoche and Pedro.

I was shown that, energetically, to bring His Holiness and Alessandro together ... the stakes were very, very high. How could His Holiness travel, in his burgundy and saffron robes, anywhere - without being highly visible and thus noticed? If His Holiness was to be a physical 'shelter' for Alessandro's awakening ... it would need to be discreet, quiet, private.

---

[10] Collective fear would need to dissipate, to dissolve sufficiently such that it would be 'unafraid' to allow the tip of the Beak to meet, these souls thus activating the re-configuring of the Dove.

I was shown then the link between Khamtrul Rinpoche ... and Pedro. Still extremely powerful. Yet not one to attract public attention. This ... this could happen. This - would be our next step.

♥

I had been shown this several times. In dreams and waking visions. I was shown ... his energetic similarity to Pedro. They - Lancelot● and Pedro - they were both pure Gabriel energies.

I had been told that Lancelot was 'waiting in the wings'. That, at the precise and appropriate Time, he would appear to 'create a bridge, a link'. That he would connect me to Pedro.

And this he did.

I had been prepared to meet Lancelot, in the physical, for several months. It was publicly known that he visited Dharamsala frequently. And so it was simply a matter of synchronicity, and Time.

The day arose, like a sun from a sea.

I was sitting with my colleagues in a Tibetan restaurant. And he walked in. He sat at a table on the other side of the room.

Agni saw him. "Give me a moment", she whispered. "I will know what to do."

I already knew.

I rose and walked discreetly to his table. I kneeled beside him. And I said.

"We have a mutual friend, Khamtrul Rinpoche."

"You know Khamtrul?" His eyes lit up.

"I'm wondering if you'd come to a private audience with him - with me", I said.

"Yes, yes!"

We agreed to meet the next day, in the large courtyard at the main temple, after the teachings.[11]

I spotted him in the crowd - not difficult, he being a westerner amongst thousands of black haired and ornately clad Tibetans in their chupas and hats.

He spotted me too.

It took him some time to extricate himself from the dozens of westerners who wanted a minute of his time. Eventually, and very graciously, he broke free, and we descended some steps and were away from the crowd.

"Let's walk", he said.

We walked at a rapid pace down a trail which led ultimately to the guest house at which he was staying, deep in the forest. As we walked, he fired questions in much the same way as the Dalai

---

[11] Each year the Dalai Lama offers public teachings at his monastery in Dharamsala. Thousands of Tibetans, and many westerners, make the pilgrimage for this.

Lama had. A rapid match of third-eye 'ping pong'. This time, in swift motion, on foot.

"You've been bitten by a bug!" he exclaimed, with an enormous grin.

"Yes, a huge bug". I smiled. Finding friends who understood - who could comprehend the scope of what I had remembered and what I was 'carrying' - were rare. I cherished every one of them.[12]

"What do you want me to do?" He asked, open, genuinely open.

"Help me to meet Pedro". I was direct.

We were silent for a few moments as we continued to walk.

"Alright. Let's meet with Khamtrul." He resumed his silence then. Our conversation had concluded. That was all ... for now.

♥

A few days later, we met with Khamtrul Rinpoche - Lancelot and I.

Agni and I had already met with Khamtrul a day before. And in that meeting, I had 'pulled energetic teeth'. We had gone to

---

[12] When I first emerged from seclusion, I felt so alone with what I 'knew'. I felt that ... if Buckminster Fuller, or Carl Jung, or Mahatma Gandhi were alive, we'd

Khamtrul to 'pitch' (the language of the movies, Agni's background) our request that he travel with me to England, to 'shelter' a meeting with Pedro.

He had agreed, though with several caveats which needed to be navigated.

"I'm so old." And ... "I don't' speak English." And ... "What could I possibly have to offer?"

With each of these 'bluffs', I had to reply with a concrete, inarguable answer. I pondered a brief moment. Then I saw it! Khamtrul and Pedro were both mystics. And poets. And philosophers. And present day shamans, too.

Khamtrul agreed. He and his son, Abhan Rinpoche, would accompany me to England.

♥

The audience with Khamtrul, Lancelot and I was one of the most delightful, 'light' experiences I had in months. This next task at hand would be arduous - invisible to most, and potent in its energy.

Lancelot helped with shining generosity to prepare Khamtrul - and me - for the journey.

The date was set to meet with Pedro.

Khamtrul, Abhan and I flew.

---

be avid friends. We'd converse and share our ideas and awarenesses! I felt, in

♥

It was strange being in England again. So much had transpired in India. I was the same person, and yet I was so new.

Julia, one of the New York wave who'd participated in the London Beak 'rehearsal' Conclave, greeted us. She'd had powerful dreams of she and Khamtrul over the years. Now, finally, she met him in the flesh. And her dreams made perfect sense.

We journeyed north, to Pedro's home village.

On the agreed upon day Khamtrul, Abhan and I walked the narrow field paths connecting our guest house with his home.

We sat, six of us in all (Khamtrul, Abhan, a translator, Pedro, his assistant, and myself), in a comfortable gathering room.

Khamtrul and Pedro spoke for some time, with the assistance of the translator. Pedro was clearly honored by Khamtrul's presence, offering him a white kata.[13] They shared experiences, and stories of their similar interests. Still, it was evident, Pedro was puzzled as to 'why we were here'.

Khamtrul picked up on this cue. It was Time. He introduced me to Pedro.

---

pondering this, so un-alone. ... Then I realized. They were all 'dead'.
[13] In Tibetan culture it is ceremonial to offer a white silk scarf - a kata - as a symbol of respect to a teacher (or a shrine of a teacher) when you are received for an audience.

I 'got out of the way' with 'my' mind, and I let my guidance lead this delicate conversation. I told Pedro select, basic details of the vision - a 'first layering'. Only what he needed to know, now.

I told him of the song - the first song that I heard him sing. And of how its lyrics assured me that he, too, 'knew'.

And I told him about Alessandro.

He asked his assistant, right there in that room, to call Alessandro. To set up a meeting.

Then he and I went for a walk on a path aside a stream.

That was one of the most incredible moments of my life.

As we walked ... it was like going back, in Time. I was simultaneously aware ... of being with Pedro, for the first time in this lifetime, in the flesh. Here on this footpath, with birds singing all around us, now. And of being *in a body, with him.* As we walked, my entire being could feel our presences together. In the shared body ... of a 'Triad'.

It was a most amazing, unusual sensation. So warm, and reassuring, and magical.

We returned to the main house. Pedro spoke with his assistant briefly, inside.

He came out to where I stood. "I'm sorry, Ariole. Alessandro's people have blocked it. He won't meet."

My inner world plummeted. My entire inner being, like a skyscraper inside my body, crashed.

Pedro and I, for the moment, said our goodbyes.

Before we left, he asked if I could write my visions for him, on paper. That night, lying on my guesthouse bed, I did what I'd done a few months before, for Denma Locho Rinpoche.

Customized, written 'for them', each time. Pedro's version, I left for him the next morning. He'd already flown away. To Spain.

The next morning, Khamtrul and I went for our last walk. Hand in hand, we strolled a narrow path.

"Never give up", he said, as he squeezed my hand. "The Buddha said, 'Never give up'."

The Next Phase, Begins

Khamtrul had now gone back to India, Pedro to Spain.

And I was here, in England.

So much had transpired, so fast - since the acceleration before seclusion, really. My life was not the same.

Pedro, Alessandro and I would clearly not be meeting in the *immediate future*.

I was staying with Julia now, in her London flat.

One morning she told me that she was being shown 'my next steps'. Later that day, I had a telephone conversation with John, the psychic who had been consulted by the London Beak people who lived in the houseboat on the Thames.

Julia and John became, during this phase, my closest friends.

John, too, had been getting messages about 'what I was next to do'. They correlated precisely with what Julia was receiving. It seemed that my guides were giving me a rest - in terms of letting two people whom I trusted very deeply, guide me 'through their flesh'.

I began by leading workshops, in London. "Dancing into Ecstasy - Dancing from *Within*". And soon thereafter, "Dancing into God - A Tantric Reawakening".

In both these series of workshops, which were avidly attended immediately by dozens of Londoners, I was guiding people how to let go of the domination of their thinking brains - and to re-access the deeper wisdom of their bodies, hearts, and spirits.

With each consecutive step in the next weeks and months, I was led farther and farther away from my former 'comfort zone'. For here in London, I was gradually being guided to become visible. Publicly visible. In my 'trance'.[1]

The movement workshops soon led into 'Psychic Awareness' classes in which I taught participants how to become aware of invisible energy.

And these led to the retreats.

---

[1] This was initially a source of anxiety for me. Prior to this, I had always been guided into a private place to be taken into trance. The London Beak 'rehearsal' Conclave had been the first exception. - Even for the conference calls, I had been physically alone. So again in London now, my guides assured me. They would begin to lead me to be in trance 'in public'. Yet they would ensure that this 'public' was all people that I was completely safe with.

Safety is a key issue when in trance. For the typical self-protection functions - through awareness of one's physical surroundings - are temporarily muted. This is why trance, in indigenous cultures, is always facilitated by a shaman - someone who both knows the terrain, and can hold a safe space. In Tibetan culture, for instance, the Oracle who goes into deep trance always has a 'helper', someone to watch out for dangers in the realm of the exposed body, and to interface with outsiders who may be present with questions. In trance, I had none of these helpers in the physical. My disincarnate guides were my shamans and my 'body guards'.

The first retreats were in Wales, in a restored stone farmhouse which had just been opened for public uses. We were its first guests.

Remote in the privacy of an immense forest, this was the perfect place for 'the work'.

I didn't know the intricacy or scope of what I was being led into in this phase of 'Time'. Not until the 'AT Group'.[2] Until then, I just followed the visions of my guidance, step by step.

The first Wales retreats were led largely in silence, wherein I assisted participants to reconnect with their deep experience of spirit. I was guided to lead 'spontaneous rituals' - as an example, the creating of masks, silent processions through the forest 'in masks', and the laying aside of these masks in a still silent, intuitive ceremony.

I was guided to lead sweat lodges, and other sacred ceremonies.

Two of these retreats took place.

When they were complete, I began to experience a niggling sense that a 'community' was about to come into being. I felt both inspiration and mild trepidation. Little did I know that collective, human psychic wounds would be opened and re-enacted. *So that they could be healed.*

---

[2] The name which the group gave to itself. It means 'Ascension Teachings'.

I was innocent to all this. To the bigger 'map' or goal or 'plan' of it. I was simply trusting the brilliant leadership of my guides.

When I put out the message that I would be sharing my visions of planetary awakening, twenty four people appeared. All I knew at the outset was that I would, in fact, share my visions. 'I' thought that the purpose of this was to catalyze their *individual* ability to see visions. Little did I - or any of us know. That we were about to awaken into *collective trance.*

I can see now that, in a way, we were all stand ins for the London Beak in this 'phase'. We were doing the next steps in the alchemical work. *Because we could.*

♥

The 'AT Group' evolved completely organically. At the end of the first weekend, in London, during which I shared my visions from a state of trance, it was clear that a next weekend was to be planned.

Several of these weekend gatherings - in which I would 'teach', speaking the wisdom of my guides - took place.

Then one of the men in the group suggested that we go on an 'unfacilitated retreat - in Wales'.

Unfacilitated turned out to mean that the entire ten day experience was orchestrated by invisible guides. None of us led. 'In the flesh.' Though we all did, internally guided to at our scripted moments in Time.

It was during this Wales Retreat, the name we naturally found ourselves calling this 'AT Group' retreat, that it became evident - that we were 're-activating the life of Jesus'. That we were, somehow, helping to heal that wound. A collective, psychic wound held in the mind of all humanity. Like the wound of the holocaust.

It became clear that, to move forward in significant steps in the evolution of collective human consciousness, together we must *heal the collective past, and long past.*

Back in seclusion, this had been explained to me on an 'individual' basis. That each of us, on conscious and unconscious levels, have to 'heal our past wounds of this lifetime, and the wounds from former lifetimes that we are still carrying'. Only through doing this will our energy be *fully present, and free to move forward.*

We can't fully wake up, pulling unresolved 'drag' from the past.

And so it became apparent, here in the Wales Retreat, that this particular configuration of people were psychologically strong and able enough to, symbolically, re-activate and re-enact certain aspects of the unhealed wounds of Jesus' lifetime.

To describe this in intricate detail would be a story in itself.

Suffice to say, for this moment here, that at the Wales Retreat I was led directly into a 'stare down' with Mephistopheles.[3]

One late afternoon, I could feel something brewing. I didn't know the details, though I knew that I was to ask people - if they felt drawn to - to join me in my tent that evening.

At a precise moment, I knew - like the moment of a birth - that I was to proceed to my tent. I entered it, tied back the flaps, and lay down.

The rest became perhaps the most grueling, terrifying experience of my adult life.

I was faintly aware of people entering, flanking me as in the past life memory of the maiden. Others who could not fit inside the tent - or who sensed that their place was outside of it - circled around.

It was as if I was being strapped down, held motionless, still. Then the face came. Before it, flew … thousands and thousands of tiny black hatchets. Thousands of them. Cold, solid, pitch, black.

They flew towards me, like rapid birds, thousands of them. Neutral like cold grey steel yet vicious in the intensity of their flight. And I, 'tied down', energetically - I could not move.

They flew towards me, at lightning speed. And only when they arrived within searing distance of my body, my face - they parted.

---

[3] He who stared Buddha down under the banyan tree.

They flew directly at me. And then they parted.

This was enormously frightening. Like a psychic persecution.

Then 'he' came. The daggers were followed by *one face.*

The blackest, darkest, most fierce and malevolent face I had ever seen.

I knew him. I recognized him only by name. He was ... 'Mephistopheles'.

He stared me down. I flinched. I tried to turn my head, to avoid his eyes. He *demanded.* That I look *directly into his eyes.*

Finally, with nowhere to escape, I did.

I looked into him, and through him. And he dissolved.

Everyone around me relaxed. Like flood waters had parted. Like fire had suddenly ceased.

I felt exhausted. Some people stayed, to linger in the fascination of what they'd witnessed, and to soothe themselves. A few people stayed, to soothe me.

Within days we were back in London. The meaning and the scope of the 'AT Group' had evidently increased.

♥

It was not long after the Wales Retreat that Tara, one of the most psychologically strong in the group, asked me to intensify it. She felt that I was holding back, catering to the fears of those less courageous.

I was relieved at her request, as I had felt this, too. Yet it had been clear to me not to 'turn up the heat' on my own decision. Just like disincarnate guidance – I, with the 'AT Group', had to be invited *by* them to 'amp up the Light'.

Within days I was shown that I was to facilitate the 'Devon Intensive'. People couldn't participate simply by wanting to. They would have to agree to basic 'rules'.

The first was that, for a week prior to the Intensive, everyone was to abstain from any substances which could dull their pure perception - alcohol, sugar, nicotine, caffeine, and any sort of drugs. I assumed that this would rule out a few.

To my amazement, virtually the whole group came.

In being prepared for the Devon Intensive, my guides had shown me the 'Map' - of the first two of the four days. They had shown me in precise detail how I was to facilitate, and what would take place. Until the end of the second day. Beyond that I, too, was blind.

The first two days were led in silence. Powerful experiences and visions were witnessed by all. The nature of a silent retreat is, in itself, very challenging and revealing for people.

On the third day, someone asked for a sweat lodge. A few people in the group had found a perfect site down by the stream on their walk the day before. I agreed.

When Lisa asked me, apparently innocently, if it was alright for her to bring her dream catcher into the lodge, I knew that a malevolent storm was brewing. I could see the 'dream catcher' acting as a vortex, a funnel, *to draw dark energy in.*

I was further alarmed when, as we were walking down the path toward the site to prepare it for the lodge, Adam was idly joking with others about 'sickles', and 'scythes'.

I recognized these as symbols of malevolence, representing very dark and dangerous forces.

Down at the site, I found myself repelled by the activity. I couldn't assist.

I discretely withdrew, conscious not to impose 'my' process onto those who seemed intent on building this lodge.

And I walked back up the hill.

There, to my surprise, I found Caitlin. And later Rob and Marsha came in. We each individually had felt that 'something mischievous was transpiring … building'. And we all had felt very clear guidance not to participate in it.

I went to bed that night. And when I awoke in the morning, my guidance was stern and severe. I was not to budge on it.

I entered the 'shrine' room - the room which we had set out for when we gathered in circles. Other times, it was to be silent, for meditation. Someone had desecrated it - strewn pillows and papers and others' sacred objects everywhere.

I gravitated to a particular place on the floor, and I sat.

Gradually, over the next few hours, people came in, one at a time. Each within moments relinquished their chatter, their inner 'buzz' and fell into silence, finding a place to sit in the growing circle.

When everyone was 'in', I said. "We are all to leave this room. And we are not to re-enter it. Until we are very, very clear. That no malevolent energies are 'piggy backing on us'."

I continued. No one had ever witnessed 'me' speak with such severity before.

"When someone re-enters this room, it will be the responsibility of all those already in it to determine if their discernment is clean - if they are in fact clear. If they are not, they must leave again.

"These are the rules." And with this, I stood and left the room.

The 'game' was over. This was serious.

From morning until pitch black of night, a vigil process was underway. People came, and were deemed 'unclear', and left again. Numerous times, those expelled would run down the side of the adjacent hill, screaming 'blue murder' as a deep and formerly hidden pain inside of them was purged. They would re-enter 'The Room', radiant and beaming.

Not all of us re-entered the room that day. Though most did.

It was after midnight by now. And a few people simultaneously voiced aloud, "Where's Adam?" Several of us sensed that 'we weren't complete - this process wasn't finished - until Adam was in'.

Suddenly, there in the darkness outside the tall glass window, he stood. Sage knew it was her role to ask him in. She did.

Adam entered the room via a door which, interestingly, no one else had taken.

He sat down, clearly agitated. He didn't seem ... like 'him'.

He shivered, and shifted his body about on the cushion on which he now sat.

"I" ... "I" ... He was trying to express something foreign to him, and apparently somewhat frightening.

"I" ... Then he became still, and solid. As if, somehow, he had 'arrived'.

"I ... am ... Lucifer."

My whole being moved so swiftly. Without me thinking, my body propelled itself across the room to where he sat.

"I am Michael", I said, soothing him, recognizing him.

Something broke in The Room.

A Timeless glow hovered about us and in us all for some time. We were not ourselves - and yet we were very much ourselves.

Day broke. Rays of light filtered through the windows. Still immersed 'in' this experience, we made our way in silence into the main house. We packed our belongings. This morning, we were to leave this place.

The buildings vacated and all of our luggage packed into the vehicles, someone led us up to a nearby knoll, for our 'closing circle'.

No one was quite sure how we were to proceed - not even me. Normally, we would have had a closing circle, to complete the energy of the Retreat, and to free us to return to the city and to our 'lives'. Our lives were becoming, more and more, this work.

Archie spoke. "I am Uriel". And the whole story began.

For the next three hours, undisturbed by anyone outside of ourselves, the most fascinating collective experience I have ever been a part of unfolded. Before our very eyes.

We each knew, by name, who we 'were'. What character we were portraying. *We were the archangels.*

We knew in intricate detail when we were to speak, to whom, and what. And what symbolic gestures we were to engage.

It was marvelous, and intriguing. We were all *in collective trance.*

Adam had split the 'seam', opening *this world* to us. Like a Shakespearean play being written *in the moment,* to be seen again by no one, witnessed only by us ...

It came to 'completion' in its own Time, each of us in our own way, stunned. We didn't comprehend yet what had happened, or why. Yet it had.

♥

In the next few months, the frequency of our gathering together intensified. Almost every second weekend, we would meet. And 'the Story', the name by which Tara and others naturally began to call this process - our awareness of the unraveling of 'Time' ... would unfold.

We had been tapped into a level of consciousness in which we became players, co-creators, in the healing *of the archangels themselves.*

We, through following the story-telling and guidance of *energy,* began to be revealed a comprehension of *how* the Grey energy 'fell'. How Time had been created. And how it was now being completed, and healed. *We were seeing this, this time, from the vantage of the archangels themselves.*

'As above, so below'.

We were being asked to assist, and in so doing we were taught, from the vantage of form, how to alchemically, energetically 'untangle' the archangels (and thus the Dove!), thus narrowing the divide between they and we. We were taught the power of *witnessing* - of seeing *what truly is*. In witnessing *truth,* illusion falls away.

It rapidly became evident that, in our lives, then, there was only a faint (if any) distinction between *three parallel levels of existence.* 'Our' lives - in the 3D flesh. The metaphoric 'Jesus lifetime' - for the purpose of its healing - *so that its snagged energy could be liberated to move forward again.* And the archangel level of existence. That ... *these three ... were the same. They were energetically identical ... on three correlating stratas of existence.*

It was a bewildering and a most fascinating time. A phase which still continues.

♥

It was during these months that the boundaries between 'our lives' and the profound energetic awakening work that we found ourselves in the heart of intensified to the greatest 'heat'.

We had clearly been forged by the trust required by our collective process. Our relationships had been challenged and strengthened. Our trust in ourselves increased. And, perhaps most importantly, our trust in the 'unseen intelligence' that was leading us on this collective journey was very strong.

This was absolutely necessary for what was about to unfold. Just as my personal trust in the 'invisible process' had been gradually strengthened as seclusion progressed, a similar 'upward arc' was now taking place within the AT Group.

We were, in three steeply graded stages, introduced to the Greys - and the Greys behind the Greys, and the blackest of black energy behind them all.

It was a most arduous, and amazing, process of the Greys trusting us. And then, those 'darker Grey' entities 'hiding behind' them ... trusting us. And then, even the darkest, hiding behind them, trusting us. 'The Room' in the Devon Intensive had prepared us with sufficient discernment and clarity of energetic boundaries for this miracle to take place.

A way of understanding the Grey energies is to recognize shame. Shame, and fear of retribution.

As the Greys realized that we, the 'AT Group', had developed the conscious ability to *assist them to transmigrate - to awaken to themselves - and to remember themselves, at Source, as Light* - they began to present themselves to us. To allow us to perceive them. To come out of hiding, as it were.

We realized that they were petrified, 'quaking' at the thought of being discovered. They knew that, in perceiving them, we would recognize all the suffering which they had sparked and propagated. And they were sure, in their belief, that we would retribute against them for this.

When one understands that Greys are distinct from Source in that they cannot feel - the strand of their original vibration which they lost in 'falling' was the capacity to feel - then it is also possible to recognize that the Greys 'eat' negative emotions. They effect tragedy and drama and suffering in order to feed on negative human emotions and conditions.

Well aware of the degree of suffering which they had elicited over Time, and existing in the ultimate magnetic pull of duality, they believed that, if ever they were 'found out' - perceived, 'seen' - that we would punish them for their 'crimes'.

What they didn't realize, perhaps before that very moment - that moment of *trusting* us enough to let us see them! Is that Light does not punish. It does not retribute. It only illuminates.

Source, Light, Love remembers all energies that have forgotten themselves. It holds an eternal space for them to remember. And when they do, no matter what Time has passed and what suffering has taken place, they welcome the 'fallen' energies back. This is the ultimate in acceptance. For, in remembering themselves as Light, *they are no longer capable of effecting suffering*. They are no longer capable of - or driven to - effecting harm.

As the 'AT Group', we had, through the initiation process which we had magically been guided through, evolved to a level of *Source* consciousness relative to the Greys. We were, in other words, more conscious or awake to *Light*, than they. Thus we were able to see them, and to forgive them. To absolve them of their 'past'.

We, as true 'volunteers', were able to welcome them 'Home'.

The Greys sensed this. With extreme trepidation at first, individual Greys led their path. Like a line of entities, one by one, from the tip of an 'iceberg' to its base, they presented themselves to our awareness. They 'came out from hiding'.

And, absolutely consistently, they experienced our *unconditional acceptance of them*. Without blame, or punishment *whatsoever*. *We welcomed them - the once self-forgotten energies, now self-remembered ... Home*.

We were able to do this, because during 'The Room' at the Devon Intensive we had been taught. We had been taught how to recognize manipulative energies. How to set an un-negotiable boundary to them. This boundary was simple, consistent, and clear.

"You are not allowed to manipulate through me."

For the Greys, as disincarnate entities, could only affect the planet by manipulating 'through' people. They needed 'pawns', malevolent channels. People who agreed, either consciously or through ignorance, to let them 'piggy back' on them, giving them access to the Earth. They had, through Time, become masters at this.

We had learned and under stood this well, apparently, at the Devon Intensive.

For now the dark, manipulative energies were coming to us in force.

When the Greys presented themselves to us, one by one, then in clusters, then in droves - and we maintained our loving boundaries, un-negotiable, clear - we began to witness their *transmigration.* An absolutely amazing sight.

As we 'watched' them - as we *witnessed their divinity,* despite *their* perception of themselves as being solely malevolent - they journeyed from manipulation … *into the Light.*

We remembered them as Light. And they became it. Again. *This is the power of witnessing - of seeing truth.* They remembered their origin. They became pure Light again.[4]

---

[4] The first Time the universe opened its mysteries and led me to witness this miracle, I was with John, the seer from London. After some time of razor-sharp, compassionate 'watching', the former 'Greys' had successfully transmigrated, remembering themselves as being originally of the Source - of *Light.* Immediately then they recognized - they awakened to - all of the suffering that they had affected. In a 'eureka' moment, they realized that they could, with the same intelligence with which they had created destruction (eg. 'the bomb'), *they could dismantle it.* Just as they had filtered in through human minds, creating destruction, *they could filter in through human minds, healing what they had created.* They could filter to humanity technologies and intelligence (consciousness) which would heal the planet - and heal the human wounds.

We thought that this was the end. Marveled by this - by what we had just experienced and witnessed, and somewhat exhausted by it - we were flabbergasted when *even darker energies began to appear.*

It became immediately evident that these, even denser energies, had 'hidden from our perception, behind the Greys'.

As always, the design of this process was brilliant. For we had, through 'The Room' at the Devon Intensive - and recently through the 'transmigration of the Greys' - become swiftly 'expert' in witnessing dark energies.

They were spooky, at first. Every time. Not the kind of 'strangers' you really want to meet.

Yet every time, *we were capable of seeing their Light behind their darkness.* We were capable of seeing their illusory truth - *their fear.*

And this gave us compassion.[5]

So we entered the second round. The 'darker' Greys. Seeing them. Setting our clear and vital 'no manipulation boundary'. And then witnessing their transmigration. Their 'laying down of their weapons of destruction', as it were. Their remembering themselves as originally being of Love. And their return, at their core and throughout their entire being, to *being* this Love.

---

[5] Fear is a very 'small' energy. It creates massive 'illusions' to hide it. Recognizing fear - *seeing* it - instantaneously disarms the illusions - and evaporates the fear itself. Then *compassion* reigns.

Again, we thought that we were finished. Even more exhausted this time, we were blown away when the blackest of the black of 'consciousness' (or lack of it) presented itself to us. Again we realized that it had hidden itself *so effectively* from our awareness - behind the darker Greys, and they behind the Greys.

We were frightened, and not, this time. For even though these were the most ultimately vicious of energies, we knew that we had the tools to assist them. And *we realized that they were finally letting us see them - **because they knew that we could assist them to return to the Light.***

Apparently, they were ready. They had witnessed those ahead of them - their courage, our unwavering acceptance, and our guiding them out of darkness, 'Home'. Gradually the most malevolent 'became lighter', light enough to trust us to let us see them, and to facilitate their ultimate, essential healing - their awakening, their remembering themselves as *Light*.

They wanted to go 'Home'. They were ready to heal. They were ready to receive Love.

Finally, after three rounds of this following the Devon Intensive - the most arduous and fascinating of our experiences together to date - this intensity was complete. The Greys had 'turned themselves inside out'. On the energy levels, the psychic war - the psychic control of the human mind - was over. Now, it would only be 'Time' ... before the results of this became evident, on Earth.

♥

One day, I knew that I was to pay Tara a private visit. There was something which she and I were to unlock, together, 'alone'. She sensed this, too.

When I arrived at her south London flat, she had adorned the space with gorgeous flowers, bowls of water, and candles. Pinks and oranges prevailed.

We sat down, each knowing and not knowing what we were about to do.

In the silence of our sitting, 'it' began.

I was channeling Jesus' voice. She was the witness, and the one to hold the space, the soothing space for this.

Jesus showed me that he was in a 'cage'. That ... he had been 'left' there. That ... when the crucifixion had taken place, all present had become immersed in 'that moment'. They were transfixed with that moment. They had become absorbed in the reactions and hysteria of the crowd. *And they forgot Him.* That ... until 'His' wound was healed. *He could not appear again.* 'He' could not move forward in Time.

Tara and I understood that Jesus was showing us both a metaphor *and* His reality.

Tara asked Him, through me, "What are we here to do? How can we help you?"

And he said, "Simply witness me". And with that, he gradually, quickly evolved from the 'cage'. Leaving it behind 'Him'.

We could feel 'His' pain wash away. He was renewed.

Later, as Tara and I rested from this intense experience, as if having been midwives, He showed us more.

He explained that the crucifixion had not been part of the 'plan'. That He had been intended, as Buddha and others, to live a full life.

That ... *His* lifetime was intended to be that of 'the mass awakening'.

But, in the midst of His teachings. His teachings which were effecting the mass enlightenment - the awakening of the 'volunteers' ... *fear* intervened. The Greys, to explain it simply, could not imagine that the mass awakening could be ... 'benign' to them. They feared their own 'death'. *They had no way of comprehending that its entire purpose was to embrace them - to reclaim them to the Whole.*

And so they aborted Him.

Alas, the 'plan' had not taken into account, sufficiently, how to keep the Greys out of fear.[6]

---

[6] This is what the collective awakening of the Waves in the Conclaves and most specifically the Caravans are ingeniously designed to do ... to create a wave of

In the moments as Jesus 'died', He released the entire 'package' of Light with which He'd come. This was experienced like intense arrows of Light, into the hearts of all those who walked the Earth. Because He had 'died' - been 'airlifted out' - long before His intended 'Time', this was such an unprecedented and potent voltage of *Light* into the human heart. The human heart wasn't strong enough for this power yet.

The 'plan' had been to gradually fortify human hearts *over the course of Jesus' full lifetime.* At His premature 'death', this was not complete. The impossible question was then - to take the Light 'out' (it would be lifetimes before the stage would be set for this again), or to blast it in an unprecedented fashion. The latter was chosen. It was not a pleasant choice.

The people, then, were not yet sufficiently prepared for the 'blast' of this Light into their hearts. This, unfortunately, became their 'fear'. Their 'shock'.

They became 'afraid' ... of the potency of *Light.*

Tara and I listened to this, in awe.

♥

Love - of benevolent consciousness - so sweeping across the globe that fear can no longer take hold.

Soon after this, I was shown that I was to make an audio recording of my 'visions'. That I was to anchor them, audibly.

Six of us went to a remote stone cottage, again in Wales. There, over the course of several days, we held the space for me to speak from trance the anchor points of my visions.

Soon after that, it was apparent that the AT Group, in physical terms, was to disband. Having all lived in London prior to this, it was as if the group 'exploded'. Like the Big Bang. Geographically, people moved to new homes in the south, the west, the east, and the north.

The 'Group' hasn't met since. Though several of us continue the work of 'unraveling the Story', very consciously. Each in the unique, alchemical, 'metaphoric ways' that we are guided to.

The birth of the 'Dove' … continues its gestation …

A New Voice Speaks

I am here.

It is Time Now.

Release the linear path. Shed the fear of the unseen. You *Know* it. You Know it more intimately than you know yourself, in this lifetime, 'now'. It is your friend. It has been your constant companion, throughout all of Time.

Listen inwards. Here you will Know All That You Need To Know. In fact ... you already Know it.

You are dependent on no one. And you are inter-dependent with All.

See the Light in every body - people, plants, creatures, stars. See their radiant *Light*. As if they are ... smiling. For Love smiles. Light smiles. This is its nature.

Do not go forward without Knowing you are called. This is the distinction between the 'past' ... and the Eternal Now. When you feel called, it is the Light calling you. When you move without this call, you are moving from the past.

This is how you free yourself from fossilization.

Learn to listen in, in every moment. No two moments are alike. No decision is permanent. Except the decision to go 'Home'.

Return to the stage of constant wonder. Everything is 'new' - every moment, every person, every opportunity. Live as if you have just arrived here, on this precious Earth. Live as if this is your only day, as if you are a visitor here, in this sacred place. When you do this, you will enter the resonant field of sacredness itself. You will remember, naturally, that you are sacred. That all Life is sacred. And you will awaken, as if having been long asleep, to recognize that all is energy ... sacred energy. You will begin to see Life beyond - beyond the perceptual limits where you thought Life ended. You will awaken ... to what *Is*.

I am here now. I am here, with you.

Do you remember me?

Do ... you remember ... 'me'?

I am your friend. Even you who may initially quake, remembering yourself as having, at some time in the 'past', been my foe. You are not my foe. I see you not as my foe. I remember you - I always have - as my kin.

Everything is precious. Live your life remembering this - recognizing this. There is nothing wasted in 'creation'. Everything has purpose, meaning. Everything ...

There is Light in all apparent 'darkness'. *See* it. *Remember* it ...

A New Voice Speaks

And you will awaken …

For no shadow can remain where there is Light.   Light within, or Light without.

For Light permeates all 'things'.   All thoughts.   And all emotions. Nothing can hide … in the presence of Light.

I am here.

I am the Light …

Afterword

S oon after this I was guided to return to India, this time to be in the quiet of the Himalayas to write the second draft of 'the book'.

I returned to England long enough to type it. And to seek a publisher. It was closer to 'the Time' to release it. Though obviously not yet.

I returned to Canada, where I was given a 'rest'. I founded a corporate consulting practice to 'bring spirit into the concrete world'. Then, after three years, I was given the guidance that *it was time to dance again!*

I returned to the stage, miraculously, after fourteen years away. I enjoyed three years of creating, performing, and solo touring, including creating an ensemble contemporary ballet in honor of the many lepers and street children I had met in my journeys.

The stage play which was written earlier this autumn was born in response to numerous questions from the audience during my recent solo tour. "What was it like to meet the Dalai Lama?" So many people asked this - *in exactly these same words.*

A few months later, this book was born. I complete this, on its sixth day of writing, on Christmas Day, 2005.

♥ Ariole K. Alei

Vancouver, Canada

Bibliography

Solara. *The Star Borne: A Remembrance for the Awakened Ones.*
Star Borne Unlimited, USA, 1989

Rushdie, Salman. *Satanic Verses.* Picador, UK, 2000

Pauls, Menno, as told to Ray Hudson. *The Gathering of the Eagles.*
Menno-Ray Publications, circulated via word of mouth, hand
to hand, 1981

About the Author

Ariole K. Alei (see www.sharonwehnerdance.com – her birth name and recent dance company) is currently a Wellness, Relationship, and Spirituality Coach, a Spiritual Match-maker, and a Therapeutic Healer. She also teaches Yoga and Meditation.

She is the co-founder, with her husband Colin Hillstrom, of *Veraxis* Coaching and Training™ and HeartSong Solutions™ including HeartSong Matchmaking™ - "the world's first holistic matchmaking service, designed specifically for personal growth oriented singles." They live in Canada.

For information on her other writings including the trilogy Awakening Instinct - the true feminine principle ♥ Running the Gauntlet – navigating our way to our fully embodied potential ♥ Windows Through Time - a 'possible evolution' story as well as HeartSong: Conversations About Love, Joy and Sex – *Discovering the Secret to a Fulfilling Love Relationship* co-authored with her husband Colin Hillstrom … and for advance notices of forthcoming titles, write ariole@veraxis.net, Subject: Writings.

For information on her classes, workshops, public speaking, and retreats, write ariole@veraxis.net, Subject: Teachings.

For information about **HeartSong Matchmaking**™, **HeartSong Couples, Families, and Teens**, write ariole@veraxis.net, Subject: HeartSong.

HeartSong Solutions™

PO 647 - 2768 West Broadway

Vancouver, BC, Canada, V6K 4P4

(604) 731-1783

Visit our websites: www.veraxis.net

www.HeartSongSolutions.ca

* * *

Speak to the New Voice.

Ask it questions.

It will answer you …